P9-CQM-252

# Deepening Youth Spirituality

## THE YOUTH WORKER'S GUIDE

### Revised & Expanded Edition of "LIVING IN THE LIGHT"

## WALT MARCUM

Abingdon Press

Nashville

# Deepening Youth Spirituality

## THE YOUTH WORKER'S GUIDE

**Revised & Expanded Edition of "LIVING IN THE LIGHT"**

# WALT MARCUM

 **Abingdon Press**

Nashville

# Deepening Youth Spirituality
## The Youth Worker's Guide

*For the youth and parents at Highland Park UMC For their commitment to growing in the faith And for their openness to new ideas*

### Acknowledgments

I would like to thank Tony Peterson, Crys Zinkiewicz, Sheila Hewitt, and Joy Thompson for their support in this project.

 **Abingdon Press**

01 02 03 04 05 06 07 08 09 00—10 9 8 7 6 5 4 3 2 1

# Contents

12.20

# INTRODUCTION

A powerful scene in Lewis Carroll's *Alice in Wonderland* wonderfully captures the predicament in which those of us who work with youth sometimes find ourselves when it comes to the topic of helping youth grow in the faith.

The scene occurs when Alice, who has made the mistake of following the rabbit down the hole and has subsequently become lost, encounters the Cheshire Cat. In the Disney cartoon version of this classic, you can see a seemingly infinite number of possible paths behind Alice and the Cat as they engage in conversation. "Would you tell me, please, which way I ought to go from here?" asks Alice. "Well," the Cheshire Cat responds, "that depends a great deal on where you want to get to." "I don't much care where," replies Alice. "Then it doesn't matter which way you go," says the Cat.

This conversation captures a fundamental truth about life—and about spirituality. The answer depends on where you want to go. What is spirituality? What is our goal when we work with youth in the church? What are we trying to accomplish through all of the activities? Depending on whom you talk to, you are likely to get a wide variety of answers. There are, many believe, many paths.

But Alice's answer cannot be our answer. She didn't really care where she was going. We do. In a world in which it seems as if there are an infinite number of choices and possibilities in life and in faith, we need to have a clear vision and understanding of where we want to go.

Those of us who work with youth have a unique privilege. We work with young people during the crucial years in which their basic faith and their commitment to God take form. During the adolescent years, we form our basic view of the world, develop our ethical values, decide what we do or do not believe, and acquire the basic shape and content of the faith that will take us through life. And, as many adults testify, during our adolescent years we have many of our key faith-shaping experiences that mold and form us. What does (or does not) happen during our adolescent years can have a far-reaching effect on our spiritual formation.

As much as we like to talk about dramatic adult conversions in our faith, the reality is that it is usually during their adolescent years that we either reach or fail to reach people.

This book is designed to be a resource for you in your work with youth, providing a basic understanding of contemporary adolescent spirituality and the basic tools for working with young people.

## *What Is Spirituality?*

If you do very much reading in the literature of spirituality, you will quickly discover that there is more than one understanding of spirituality. Three understandings stand out because of their impact on our contemporary understanding.

### 1. Mystical Spirituality

In the mystic understanding of spirituality, the goal is to experience union or oneness with God. This is done by turning from the world and turning inward. God is not found or experienced in the world around us. Rather, God is experienced within our inner life. The tools of mystical spirituality include meditation and contemplation.

There is nothing distinctly Christian about this view. Nor is it distinctly unchristian. Mysticism is found in most of the world's major religions and has a long heritage within the Christian faith. This book will include some spiritual disciplines drawn from this tradition, although most youth find it difficult to get into this form of spirituality.

### 2. Classical Spirituality

A second understanding of spirituality is one in which we seek God by turning from "the world, the flesh, and the devil." In other words, we grow spiritually by turning from this (physical) world to the other (spiritual) world. The key to this type of spirituality is avoidance and disengagement. This form of spirituality often reflects a long series of don'ts. This form of spirituality also has a long heritage within the Christian faith, but it is really grounded in a neo-Platonic understanding of the universe as having two antithetical realms, physical and spiritual. We seek one realm by fleeing the other.

### 3. Relational or Incarnational Spirituality

As influential as the first two understandings have been within the Christian faith, this book is primarily based on a third understanding of spirituality. This form could be called relational or incarnational spirituality. Take a look at the following story from the ministry of Jesus:

**Luke 10:25-28**

[25] Just then a lawyer stood up to test Jesus. "Teacher," he said, "what must I do to inherit eternal life?" [26] He said to him, "What is written in the law? What do you read there?" [27] He answered, "You shall love the Lord your God with all your heart, and with all your soul, and with all your strength, and with all your mind; and your neighbor as yourself." [28] And he said to him, "You have given the right answer; do this, and you will live."

What must we do to inherit eternal life? The answer Jesus gives is that we must love. We must love both God and our neighbor. These two cannot be separated or played against each other. For, according to Matthew, Jesus follows up the love commandment by reminding us that "On these two commandments hang all the law and the prophets" (Matthew 22:40).

## *Relational Spirituality and Faith Maturity*

According to Jesus, our spirituality is expressed in relationship—in our relationship with God and in our relationship with our neighbor. In other words, our spirituality is fundamentally relational. It is also incarnational in that it is "enfleshed" or expressed in the way we live our lives.

This relational understanding of spirituality is fundamentally different from both mystical spirituality and classical spirituality. We do not become spiritual by fleeing this world, either by turning inward (mystical spirituality) or by turning away (classical spirituality). Rather, our spirituality is expressed in our lives and in our relationships.

Our faith calls us into relationship with God and with others. Behind all of our techniques and activities for spiritual growth, we have one overriding concern: to develop a personal relationship with God through Jesus Christ and relationships with our neighbors. The ultimate goal of spiritual growth is nothing less than the fulfillment of Jesus' great commandment to love God with all our heart, mind, soul, and strength, and our neighbor as ourselves. When we study the Bible, pray, worship, or engage in any spiritual exercise, this overriding goal is behind that activity.

### Growing Into the Full Stature of Christ

But we can take this a step further. What is the goal of our spiritual growth or formation? The apostle Paul gives us an insight into this question in the following passage from Ephesians:

**Ephesians 4:11-16**

[11] The gifts [God] gave [the church] were that some would be apostles, some prophets, some evangelists, some pastors and teachers, [12] to equip the saints for the work of ministry, for building up the body of Christ, [13] until all of us come to the unity of the faith and of the knowledge of the Son of God, to maturity, to the measure of the full stature of Christ. [14] We must no longer be children, tossed to and fro and blown about by every wind of doctrine, by people's trickery, by their craftiness in deceitful scheming. [15] But speaking the truth in love, we must grow up

in every way into him who is the head, into Christ, 16 from whom the whole body, joined and knit together by every ligament with which it is equipped, as each part is working properly, promotes the body's growth in building itself up in love.

According to Paul, the goal of our spiritual growth is nothing less than maturity, spirituality maturity. And this maturity is measured in terms of "the full stature of Christ." The goal of our spirituality is to become more like Christ, to "grow up in every way into him who is the head, into Christ."

We have a very specific goal in youth work. Our ultimate goal is what John Wesley would call "scriptural holiness" or "perfection"—that we would be "perfect in love." Our real goal is for the youth to become mature, committed disciples of Jesus Christ—to be more Christlike.

But there is one more question that needs to be answered. What is a mature faith actually like? Almost everyone in the church can agree that we are called to faith maturity and to be more like Christ, but do we really have an idea of what a mature faith actually looks like?

### Search Institute's Definition of Faith Maturity

Several years ago, Search Institute conducted a massive landmark study on faith maturity. One of the results of this study was a working definition of *faith maturity* that has received widespread support. This information has been available since the spring of 1990 and is covered in great detail in the book *The Teaching Church: Moving Christian Education to Center Stage,* by Eugene C. Roehlkepartain and Donald L. Griggs (Abingdon Press, 1993; ISBN 0687410835).

Search Institute's definition of faith maturity is fundamentally relational and is anchored firmly in Jesus' dual love commandment. According to Search Institute, there are two dimensions to faith maturity: the vertical dimension (our relationship with God) and the horizontal dimension (our relationship with our neighbor). Our faith may be strong or weak in either dimension. But a mature faith is strong and developed in both dimensions. So far, this definition just reiterates Jesus' dual commandment. But Search Institute goes further to map out the following eight characteristics of a mature faith:

## *Eight Expressions of a Mature Faith*

### 1. Trusting and Believing

A person with mature faith trusts in God's saving grace and believes firmly in the humanity and divinity of Jesus. This affirmation is more than just intellectual content; he or she experiences God's guidance in daily life. There is a vibrant and personal relationship.

### 2. Experiencing the Fruits of Faith

A person with mature faith experiences a sense of personal well-being, security, and peace. This is what John Wesley called "Christian assurance" and what the apostle Paul called "the fruits of the Spirit."

## 3. Integrating Faith and Life

A person with mature faith integrates faith and life, seeing work, family, social relationships, and political choices as part of one's religious life. Faith is the filter through which a person views everything else in life. A mature faith is wholistic, integrated.

## 4. Seeking Spiritual Growth

That which is not growing is either stagnant or dying. A person with mature faith seeks spiritual growth through study, reflection, prayer, and discussion with others. He or she knows that faith cannot be static; rather, faith is a journey and changes must be affirmed.

## 5. Nurturing Faith in Community

God has called us into community, not to a life of isolation. A person with mature faith seeks to be part of a community of believers in which people give witness to their faith and support and nourish one another. Faith is nurtured in community; it develops as we keep company with other believers.

## 6. Holding Life-Affirming Values

A person with mature faith holds life-affirming values, including a commitment to racial and gender equality, an affirmation of cultural and religious diversity, and a personal sense of responsibility for the welfare of others.

## 7. Advocating Social Change

A person with mature faith advocates social and global change to bring about greater social justice. The Christian faith is not a passive faith; the church belongs in the public sphere.

## 8. Acting and Serving

A person with mature faith serves humanity, consistently and passionately, through acts of love and justice. Advocating social change is not enough; the person of faith becomes personally involved in serving. He or she moves beyond benevolence (wishing good) to beneficence (doing good), putting his or her faith into action.

What is our ultimate goal in spiritual growth? What are we trying to accomplish? Search Institute has given us some concrete handles on the qualities of a mature faith, but there are some other issues we need to examine.

## *Characteristics of Relational Spirituality*

In addition to being fundamentally relational, contemporary spirituality has several other important characteristics.

### 1. Relational spirituality is this-worldly rather than other-worldly.

There is no doubt that at times in our history, spirituality has focused on escaping the world we live in and has focused on a world other than this one. This classical view, which drew heavily on the neo-Platonic view of two realities, one physical and one spiritual, has been and continues to be extremely influential.

In contrast, contemporary relational spirituality is this-world oriented. Through our spiritual disciplines, we develop our relationship with God here and now. We also develop our relationships with those around us. We do not seek to take youth out of the world. Rather, we seek to have young people encounter and experience the living God, who is very much present in our world, and to engage them more fully in this world in which God is at work.

## 2. Relational spirituality is experiential rather than cognitive.

Spirituality has at times been closely identified with the cognitive and the rational. We study; we memorize; we discuss. In short, we approach God and our spirituality much as we would any other topic or subject. The result has been that we sometimes have focused more on learning about God than experiencing and developing a relationship with God.

The problem is that we can know a lot *about* God and never actually *know* God or *engage in relationship* with God. Clearly, our faith calls us to move beyond *knowledge about* to relationship with. The spirituality advocated in this book focuses on direct encounters with God and the nurturing of our relationship with God. God is not a topic to be studied. God is a living reality in our midst, whom we need to encounter and experience directly. We need a dynamic, living relationship, not just an understanding.

## 3. Relational spirituality is more concerned with relationship than with religion.

At its worst, religion can become a substitute for faith, or even a barrier to faith. Our religious practices can become ends in themselves. A healthy spirituality seeks to develop relationships. Religious practices and activities are merely tools to assist in that goal. It is not enough to go through the motions of spirituality or to have just the form of religion. Our goal is the relational substance of the faith.

## 4. Relational spirituality is more corporate than private.

Christian spirituality is essentially and fundamentally communal. Relationship requires others. At times it is helpful to pull away to "a place apart," as Jesus did. But this is not the norm. Our faith is lived in the midst of others, not apart from them. Our relationship with God and our experience of God have a strong corporate component. This element is especially true for youth. We may pull aside from time to time. We may use techniques that require us to turn inward. But the reason we do this is to strengthen us so that we can reengage the world.

## 5. Relational spirituality is more positive than negative.

An old jingle expresses a perverted view of spirituality, which still plagues the Christian community: "Don't smoke. Don't cuss. Don't chew. Don't mess around with them folk that do." All of us have run into this attitude in one way or another. The danger here is the implication that we can grow in our faith and our relationship with God simply by avoiding certain things. This thinking is fundamentally negative in its approach. A healthy spirituality is more positive than negative. While it is true that there are many harmful things we need to avoid, the real focus in spiritual growth is on the positive ways we can develop our relationship with God and make ourselves more open to God. Even if we are successful in avoiding everything that is negative, that is not enough. Developing a Christlike love for God and neighbor requires much more.

## 6. The driving image for relational spiritual growth is formation.

Being Christian is not "natural." It does not just happen. Promoting Christian spirituality is not just a matter of being age appropriate and allowing the young person's natural development to take place. Christians are made, not born. We must be taught, shaped, molded, and slowly formed into the image of Christ. This transformation is a lifelong process in which we are influenced by forces outside of us. Our parents, family, friends, and faith community all play a role.

## 7. Spiritual growth is a process, not an event.

Mountain-top experiences are wonderful, and they can play a key role in our spiritual development. But spiritual growth itself is a process, not an event. Theologically, spirituality has to do with what the apostle Paul calls "sanctification," or "going on to perfection." Growth involves change. It is dynamic rather than static. And it involves every aspect of our lives, as well as every moment. Like the apostle Paul, we press on toward the goal of perfect love.

## 8. Spiritual growth requires discipline.

Faith maturity is not a product of physical, age-related maturity. Spiritual growth or formation requires intentionality. It has always involved spiritual "disciplines," engaging in certain activities to open ourselves to God's presence in our lives. It requires spiritual "exercises," activities that must be practiced. No one is arguing that God can't work without Scripture, prayer, and worship. But it is also true that these disciplines have proved to be valuable tools for countless Christians throughout the ages. It's helpful to remember that even Jesus' disciples had to ask him to "teach us how to pray." Prayer was and is a skill that must be developed through discipline.

## 9. Spirituality requires time.

Spirituality deals with the sum total of our spiritual experiences across our entire lives. Spirituality can't he rushed; we can't make it happen. We can provide only the opportunities and the openness that enable God to work within us. It would be nice to think that there are some magical shortcuts to spirituality. We are tempted to look for the magic Bible study, prayer activity, or camp experience that somehow will make the youth we work with suddenly more spiritual. However, like any discipline, spirituality takes time.

Faith is a journey. The young people with whom we work have not arrived. They are in process, on the journey. Youth are, by definition, immature. Prominent in the New Testament is the image of discipleship as a journey moving toward the goal of perfection. Among the passages that stress this image are the following:

### Philippians 3:12-14

[12] Not that I have already obtained this or have already reached the goal; but I press on to make it my own, because Christ Jesus has made me his own. [13] Beloved, I do not consider that I have made it my own; but this one thing I do: forgetting what

lies behind and straining forward to what lies ahead, [14] I press on toward the goal for the prize of the heavenly call of God in Christ Jesus.

**Hebrews 12:1-2**
[1] Therefore, since we are surrounded by so great a cloud of witnesses, let us also lay aside every weight and the sin that clings so closely, and let us run with perseverance the race that is set before us, [2] looking to Jesus the pioneer and perfecter of our faith.

## 10. Relational spirituality is God's act.

Salvation is "by grace, through faith"; so is spiritual growth. So far we have focused on the "through faith" part of what we do. Spiritual growth does require work on our part. It requires intentionality, discipline, and practice. But we need to remember that spiritual growth is also "by grace." Which is exactly why John Wesley referred to these spiritual disciplines as "means of grace." Ultimately, spiritual growth occurs through God's prevenient grace, which is at work in our lives. Through the Holy Spirit, God moves and works within us, shaping, molding, forming, trans-forming us into the image of Christ. The divine-human relationship is synergistic—an interactive cooperation in which God is at work but also in which God invites us to be at work.

## *So, What Works?*

Assuming that we know where we want to go, how do we get there? What works? For the past several years, I have done a three-step exercise with adults who work with youth, called "A Spiritual Autobiography." Using a chart or graph format that looks like an EKG or an EEG, people first map out their life stories, the highs and lows of their lives, the significant people, events, experiences, and so forth. Then they do an overlay and map out their faith journeys: their spiritual highs and lows, the significant people, events, and experiences. Finally, they look back over their lives and their faith journeys and identify the key "faith shapers"—those things that have had a profound shaping effect on their faith and have made them who they are today as people of faith.

I never cease to be amazed by the consistency of the answers. The pattern does not vary from place to place. And it has not shifted in over ten years of doing this exercise. So, what do our own faith stories tell us are the faith shapers? What actually works? Three factors stand out.

The first is relationships. The single most consistent and powerful faith shaper in people's lives is other people: a pastor, a youth, a leader, a parent, a Sunday school teacher. The list is endless. Our faith is fundamentally relational. God invites us into relationship with God and with others. How do we grow in this relational faith? Through relationships. We learn about and grow in relationships through our experiences in relationship. The most powerful faith-shaping tools we have are not the latest gimmick, book, or idea. We ourselves are what is important. Years after youth have left our programs, they may remember little of what we have said. What they will remember is the quality of the relationship.

The second factor that stands out time and again is experiences: a camp, a worship service, time alone, DISCIPLE BIBLE STUDY, the Walk to Emmaus. Again, the list is endless. But it is consistent. Time and again, significant experiences have a profound effect on our faith. Sometimes it is the stuff of life: divorce, death, and other tragedies. These boundary experiences are often pivotal. Yet their effect can be either helpful or destructive. The difference seems to be in the way they are handled. At other times, the experiences are explicitly religious in nature. Whenever possible, we want to provide, create, or enable experiences that have the potential to be life and faith shaping.

The third factor is the power of "the means of grace," the classic disciplines of the faith: Bible study, prayer, worship, the sacraments. These have a tried-and-true quality to them. They work. They open us to God's grace in powerful ways.

This book is predicated on these three faith shapers: relationships, experiences, and the classic disciplines of the faith.

## *Understanding Adolescent Spirituality*

Adolescent spirituality is not fundamentally different from any other spirituality. The difference is that, in youth work, our context is the realities and needs of youth. Adolescent spiritual growth is linked to adolescent development. As we grow, more things become possible. We work with young people during the period when they undergo the most profound changes in their lives. Their brains develop; their bodies change; their capacity to think undergoes a dramatic shift; their world broadens. All of these changes affect their spiritual growth.

The teen years provide challenges as well as opportunities. Adolescents do not have a fully formed or developed faith. They can be immature. They do not have a great depth of experience and understanding from which to draw. Adolescence is a time of questioning and challenging. Teenagers will critique and test the faith they have inherited from their families and faith community. They are also inconsistent. They compartmentalize. One minute you believe that a young person—or a group— is on the verge of the kingdom of God. The next minute you believe the opposite.

But the opportunities far outweigh the challenges. Young people are open to new experiences and activities. They are eager to learn, experience, and grow. They will engage in activities that few adults would even consider. They readily see God and Jesus as friends or buddies. Youth ministry opportunities place them in situations where great mountain-top experiences can happen. And often, we are there with them during these moments.

## *The Youth Worker's Personal Spiritual Development*

A word needs to be said about the personal spiritual growth of the adults who work with youth. There is an old truism in the counseling profession: You can't take a counselee further than where you are yourself. It's difficult for the person being helped to become healthier than the counselor or therapist with whom he or she works.

This maxim is true in spiritual growth as well. How can we expect youth to grow in our ministries if we ourselves are not growing spiritually as well? It's not a matter of our being spiritual giants. But it is a matter of our being in a living, dynamic relationship with God. Spiritual growth cannot be reduced to a series of tricks, gimmicks, or activities. Our relationship with God and our relationships with the youth have a direct bearing on our ability to work with them in the area of spiritual growth.

Our most powerful tool in working with youth is our own relationship with God. We need to be actively working to grow in that relationship through Bible study, prayer, worship, and the other disciplines. The youth we work with can sense this in us. If our relationship with God is alive and dynamic, it will show. And the youth we work with will want to experience what we have experienced. In the same way, we need to be growing in our relationship with our neighbors. We meet Christ in the midst of human need and in the midst of our human relationships.

## What Is in This Book?

This book is a resource manual, short on theory and long on practical advice. It is written by a youth worker and draws on more than thirty years' experience in working with youth. This resource seeks to bring together in one place a lot of practical, proven ideas and techniques from a wide variety of sources.

**Chapter 1** explores using Bible study with youth as a key to developing a relationship with God. It covers the importance of the Bible for spiritual growth, some basic guidelines for Bible study with youth, and several tried-and-true Bible study techniques.

**Chapter 2** deals with active prayer (speaking to God). It explores a basic understanding of the nature of prayer, some practical suggestions for prayer with youth, and 24 prayer activities that work well with youth.

**Chapter 3** presents a special type of prayer often neglected in contemporary youth ministry—dispositional prayer. It focuses on learning how to listen to God, not just speak to God. This type of prayer is particularly appropriate for youth in developing a relationship with God. After covering the components of dispositional prayer, the remainder of the chapter is devoted to specific dispositional prayer techniques.

**Chapter 4** examines worship with youth. It includes a definition of worship and the basic characteristics of Christian worship. The bulk of the chapter deals with (1) involving youth in Sunday morning worship; (2) special "Youth Sunday" worship services; (3) youth-planned and youth-led worship for Sunday evenings; (4) worship on trips and special occasions; and (5) forming a youth worship committee. It also contains several examples of youth-planned and youth-led worship services and devotions.

**Chapter 5** is new to this edition, celebrating the growth of small groups for spiritual formation. This chapter introduces the spiritual growth potential that small groups offer. You will find tips for small group success and 20 specific discussion and activity ideas.

**Chapter 6** pulls together a lot of additional or special spiritual-growth techniques: spiritual mentoring, journaling, spiritual autobiographies, dreamwork, music, fasting, depth discipleship training, mission and service, and the role of moral values and ethical decision-making in spiritual growth.

**Chapter 7** offers a complete three-day spiritual-life retreat, which uses many of the ideas in this book. Use the retreat as written, borrow ideas from it, or use it to stimulate your own thinking.

**Chapter 8** is also new to this edition and includes a series of powerful faith-shaping exercises. In youth ministry, we sometimes refer to "silver bullets," powerful tools that help us accomplish a goal. This new chapter contains eight silver bullets that have been collected over a number of years.

God invites us into a living relationship. Spirituality is not just a part of who we are; it is who we are. Spirituality is holistic and all-encompassing. Loving God with all our heart, mind, soul, and strength, and our neighbor as ourselves, involves every aspect of our lives.

Spirituality is also a lifelong journey—a journey of faith, a life of walking in the light of God's love and grace. It is our privilege to be there with young people during the critical years in which they begin to take responsibility for their own journey, the years that are so crucial to shaping their faith.

In the midst of our work with youth, we often find that our work stimulates and enhances our own spiritual growth. Our personal walk with God is—and will continue to be—the key to our work with youth. Our own spiritual growth is our best resource as we seek to invite young people to join us in a living relationship with God in Christ. Without that underlying relationship, everything in this book is just mechanics.

Spirituality cannot be taught academically; it must be experienced, lived. Our task as role models and mentors is to invite. Our joy is to be companions on the journey.

Acting as role models and mentors requires a great deal of trust on our part. Often, we are not there to see how the journey turns out—we see relationships begin but have no opportunity to see them develop beyond the senior year in high school. We must trust God. We need a good understanding of the Holy Spirit, one that enables us to trust that God is at work in the lives of the young people we work with and will bring our efforts to fruition.

# CHAPTER

# *BIBLE STUDY*

**M**any have a mistaken idea of how today's youth react to Bible study. It runs something like the now famous scene from the teen classic movie *Ferris Bueller's Day Off*: A boring teacher drones on and on in a monotone voice as the students stare glassy-eyed into nothingness. Some students doodle on paper. Others roll their eyes. One student's head slowly slips down and finally falls to the desk.

Actually, the opposite is true. As the quotations above indicate, many of today's youth do not have a problem with Bible study. Youth hunger for the Bible and for what it can offer. The problem is not with the Bible but with how Bible study is sometimes done.

*"To me, the Bible is a very personal thing. It provides spiritual growth and a sense of comfort. It is like a window, providing a glimpse into another world and another time. It makes me feel secure knowing that my religion has survived through all the years. I compare myself to those in all the stories and wonder if I have a strong enough faith to deal with the problems they faced."*

Courtney, age 15

*"The Bible is all you really have. There are a lot of bad ideas going around and a lot of false teachers. The Bible is from God. It's been tried, and it's true. Everything else will go, but God's Word will always remain—and remain the truth."*

Ben, age 16

## *Bible Study Does Not Have to Be Boring*

The issues and concerns of Scripture are timeless. They are the stuff of life. The Bible is full of controversial and interesting topics: dysfunctional families, murder, rape. The soap operas have nothing on the Bible. And woven throughout this all-too-human narrative is the eternal truth of God for our lives.

In fact, a lot of innovative Bible-study techniques work well with teenagers. One source of great ideas is *Show Me the Way: 50 Bible Study Ideas for Youth,* by Todd Outcalt (Abingdon Press, 2000; ISBN 068709562X). These approaches are interesting and help youth delve into the Scriptures in exciting and meaningful ways. Here are some examples of others:

- In one church, a small group of students meet in a home after school. They hurry to fit in time to study the Bible between school and their evening activities. They spend an hour and a half viewing a videotape, discussing Scriptures they have read during the week, exploring how those apply to their lives, and growing closer to one another. They are a part of a DISCIPLE Bible study group for youth.

- In another church, a group of young people gathers for an experiential reconciliation exercise as part of an evening youth program. They begin in a circle, with arms linked. But as members mention various actions that separate people from one another and from God, they drop their arms, take several steps back, turn around, and close their eyes. As they stand alone in the darkness, they experience the brokenness and separation of our world.

  After a few moments, the process is reversed; participants mention behaviors and attitudes that unite people with one another and with God. The members of the group take several backward steps toward the center, turn around, and open their eyes to find themselves where they started. As they link arms, someone reads a passage of Scripture that speaks of God's desire for reconciliation. After the exercise, the group discusses things that separate them from others and from God and how God's desire for reconciliation can make a difference.

- In a Sunday school class, the students are invited to lie on the floor and close their eyes. The teacher then takes them on a guided meditation on the Nicodemus story, in John 3:1-11. With the teacher's help, the students relive the story as if they were there. They place themselves in the story and use their five senses to experience what it was like to be there. Through the meditation, each student becomes a character in the story. What happens in the story happens to them. After the meditation, the class members compare experiences and discuss what they learned from the experience.

- In countless churches across our country, youth awaken before the crack of dawn so that they can attend a Bible study with their peers who meet before school.

The list goes on and on. There are innovative, exciting ways to do Bible study with youth. The purpose of this chapter is to give you the tools you will need for such Bible study. These include understanding why the Bible is so important for spiritual growth, what is age appropriate for youth, and how we approach the Bible. A set of guidelines is included. But most of the chapter will be devoted to going over specific Bible study techniques that work with youth. At the end of this book, you will find a brief bibliography that will point you to additional resources.

## *Why Is the Bible So Important for Spiritual Growth?*

Some people might consider this question unnecessary. All of us know the answer. Or do we? Do we really know what it is that we want to see happen in the lives of young people and how the Bible can play a role in making this happen? In many settings, Christian education goes on with little or no significant contact with Scripture. The Scripture, if it is brought in at all, is almost an afterthought. In other settings, a great deal of attention is given to memorization and learning the facts or truths of Scripture. But even this emphasis may make little or no difference in a young person's life.

What is the real role of the Bible in developing our relationship with God and in growing in our discipleship and commitment to Christ?

## *What Is the Bible?*

The Bible is history, poetry, theology, story, biography, and much more. These different types of writing are important for spiritual growth.

The Bible is the church's book. It is our memory as a community of faith. It records the events that gave rise to our faith. What we know about Jesus, about God, and about what it means to be a Christian is found in the Bible. If we want to be in a relationship with God, we turn to the Bible to know more about God. If we wish to be faithful disciples of Jesus Christ, we turn to the Bible to learn more about Jesus and what he expected from his disciples. It is, in short, our primary source of knowledge about God and the how we are to respond to God's love.

The Bible contains the Word of God. Revelation can come in many ways and through many different means: a sunset, the wind, a worship service, a group of friends, a beautiful piece of music. But for the Christian community, the clearest revelation of God and of God's will for our lives is found in Scripture. To attempt to understand God's will for our lives without referring to Scripture and its witness makes no sense in the Christian community. To quote the Articles of Religion of the Episcopal and United Methodist churches, Scripture "contains everything necessary unto salvation." The Scripture is where we find *Life* with a capital *L*.

The Bible is the sufficient rule for faith and practice. The Christian community has always insisted that the Bible contains what we need to know and believe (faith) and what we need to do (instructions for life). The faithful disciple shapes faith and life in dialogue with the Scripture.

The Bible is a powerful tool for spiritual formation. Countless Christians across the ages attest to the power of Scripture to shape, mold, form, and transform the reader. We are called to be transformed into the image of Christ, and God through the Holy Spirit continues to use Scripture to do so.

## *What Does the Bible Offer?*

What does the Bible offer us for spiritual growth? The Bible contains so much that we can sometimes get lost in it. Even a brief passage may contain many different dimensions and levels of truth.

Often we get sidetracked by questions and issues with which the Bible is not really concerned. Did an event really happen? Was the world really made in six days? If so, and the sun wasn't created until the fourth day, how long were the first three days? If Adam and Eve were the only people God created, where did Cain's wife come from? Did Adam have a navel? The list is endless.

Dr. W.J.A. Power, an Episcopal priest and seminary professor, has a way of cutting to the core of what the Bible is all about. Dr. Power believes that we can get to the heart of any biblical passage by asking three simple questions:

What does it say about God?
What does it say about us as human beings?
What does it say about our relationship with God?

The Bible is primarily concerned with relationships: our relationship with God and our relationships with one another. When Jesus summarizes the commandments, he reduces hundreds of rules and regulations to two: love God and love your neighbor. In other words, Jesus reduces the complexity of the faith down to its essence: relationship.

Spirituality, at its essence, is relationship—relationship with God and with our neighbor. The Bible, at its essence, is a narrative of the relationship between God and God's people. It also contains what God has to say about relationship. It is concerned with how we grow, develop, and nurture our relationships. The biblical word is *covenant,* and covenant is all about relationship. At its very core, the Bible is the story of God's relationship with the people of Israel, and later with the new Israel, the church.

## *Age-Appropriate Bible Study*

Of the various dimensions of the Christian faith, the one adolescents are most open and receptive to is that of relationship. The teen years revolve around relationships. Relationships dominate the personal agenda of young people. Teenagers are open to and ready for an understanding of what it means to be in relationship with God and with one another. During the teenage years the relational agenda that is natural for youth coincides with the relational agenda of the Bible.

Knowing where people are developmentally is helpful in Bible study. Each stage of life has its own issues and concerns, and the Bible speaks to each of these. Be aware of where a group is developmentally and what its issues are. Basing a junior-high study on abstract theological concerns is probably not a productive activity and may give those young people the false impression that the Bible does not have anything to say to them.

Although any rule has its exceptions, age-oriented trends may dictate the issues that interest youth:

**Middle/Junior high school students (6th, 7th, and 8th grades)** are especially concerned with interpersonal relational issues. When allowed to pick the topics they wish to discuss, youth of this age group most often choose the topics that concern relationships—with parents, with peers, with God. Sex, sexuality, and relationships between guys and girls are also important. This age focuses on identity formation. The key question is, "Who am I?" When the Bible is used as a resource for dealing with these issues, junior high students are eager to learn.

**Mid-high students (9th and 10th grades)** often have a different agenda. Their world has begun to broaden, and they are concerned about issues in the world. This age, more than any other, is concerned with controversial topics: suicide, homosexuality, the devil, cults, and the occult. Moral and ethical issues move to the center. There is concern about what is right and what is wrong—and why. This group, more than any other, wants to know what the Bible and our faith have to say about these topics.

**Senior high students (11th and 12th grades)** are increasingly interested in their place in the larger adult world, with what happens after high school. Their core issues include career, separation from parents, living on their own, marriage, personal finances. Deep theological and faith concerns also become important: Is there really a God? How do I know? Is Jesus really the way? At this age, many youth begin to explore what it means to have a personal relationship with God and with Jesus Christ.

These descriptions are generalizations. All the concerns mentioned are present in each age group, but certain issues tend to be in the forefront with each. The approaches mentioned in this chapter can be used with all of these age groups, but it is helpful to keep these general trends in mind. Having a good technique is only half of the success in a Bible study with youth. The other half lies in what is called "the teachable moment"—dealing with an issue that is of genuine concern to the group. This means being age appropriate.

## Guidelines for Approaching the Bible With Youth

As you use each of the approaches in the remainder of this chapter, a few simple guidelines will help to keep the Bible study focused in a way that will enhance spiritual growth:

### 1. Provide Opportunities, Not Answers

Sometimes providing answers is appropriate. But most of the time in youth work, providing opportunities—to explore, to encounter, to question and challenge—is more appropriate. The adolescent shapes his or her beliefs and life through testing and searching. If we can provide a flexible, safe context in which young people can explore and think through their own faith, we can help them grow in their relationship with God.

If we can also provide opportunities to directly experience God's presence in the midst of life, we can take this growth a step further. Many of us remember powerful "camp experiences" when God felt very real and present. One of the challenges in youth ministry is to structure what we do in such a way that teenagers not only have an opportunity to learn about God but also to experience God. Several of the ideas in this chapter are designed to create such times.

## 2. Seize Teachable Moments

The young people with whom we work are sometimes more open and receptive than at other times. These open times are called "teachable moments." Most of the time, the students may not care about a particular truth or point. But then, with little or no warning, a teachable moment will present itself. If a suicide has happened at the local high school that week, the planned Sunday school lesson may be of little or no value. What the class needs, and what the students probably will want to do, is to talk about their feelings of loss and try to make sense of the event. At an appropriate moment, the class members may be very open to something the Bible has to say about life, death, and God's presence in these events, especially if the message is presented in a personal, relational way.

## 3. Be Open-Ended

Whose agenda do we pursue when we use the Bible with youth? Who decides what is important and what isn't? We know what the Bible says to us, and it's natural to assume that the Bible says the same thing to everyone else. The problem is that it doesn't work that way.

Teenagers are keenly aware of what teachers—in the public-school system and in the church—want. They know how to play the game of giving the answer that is expected. There is an old joke about a junior high student who was sitting in Sunday school class and not really paying attention to what was going on. The teacher was trying to find out when a particular event would be happening at the local middle school. The teacher asked the student if he knew. Startled, he responded, "I didn't really hear what you asked, but I know that the answer you want is Jesus." Adolescents can easily give back the expected answers, and after they go out the door, never have another thought about what was said.

The object of spiritual growth is different. If our goal is to develop a relationship with God and our neighbor and to grow in those relationships, then what we learn needs to shape our lives: our values, our attitudes, our behavior, our decisions, our beliefs. This shaping is intensely personal for each individual. Youth do not need our faith. What they need is to develop their own faith and their own personal relationship with God.

For this to happen, youth must internalize the content of the Scriptures. Its truths must become their truths. The Story must become their story. The God revealed there must become the God who is alive and at work within their world and their lives. We must allow each young person to struggle with the Scripture in his or her own way. We can set up the opportunity for encounter, but the encounter itself will be different for each person.

We can't presuppose that our answers will be adolescents' answers. They may look at a particular passage (or at the Bible as a whole) in a different way than we do. Various interpretations of Scripture have always existed within the Christian community. One person takes a passage literally. Another sees spiritual truths in the passage. Still others see it as story that speaks to them.

When we work with youth, we can't expect everyone to have the same pat answer. If we believe that the Holy Spirit is at work in each person, then we must accept that the Holy Spirit may work in different people in different ways. When we study the

24

Bible, youth may not see what we see. Our answer may not be their answer. They may see something that we have missed. Their answer may teach us something we didn't know about God or about ourselves.

As we work with youth, we need to provide opportunities to encounter God, not just teach information about God. Relationship remains primary. The call to discipleship is a call to relationship. A person can know a lot about God without actually knowing God. By trusting the youth with whom we work, the Bible, and the Holy Spirit, we can free ourselves from the desire to control the process. Instead, we can allow God to use us and the Scripture as each individual slowly develops his or her unique relationship with God.

## 4. Use Both Sides of the Brain

Modern research has indicated that each side of the human brain performs a different function. The left side is analytical and logical. The right side is intuitive and artistic. Too often, Bible study has been limited to left-brain approaches. The Bible is more than a collection of intellectual propositions to be memorized and adhered to. In addition to left-brain approaches, such as memorization and deductive study, we need to incorporate inductive Bible study approaches that are experiential, relational, and intuitive. These right-brain approaches work particularly well with youth. Inductive approaches include the use of motion, art, narrative story, and direct experience.

## 5. Be Experiential

One of the insights of contemporary educational theory is that different people learn in different ways. Some are visually oriented; others are more auditory; and still others are more kinesthetic, learning more through movement. Another insight is that different approaches to learning can have a different impact. The most direct and powerful form of learning is experiential. If someone tells us something, we may or may not believe it. And even if we do believe, what he or she says may make little or no difference in our lives. However, when we ourselves experience something, it has a direct and powerful impact on us. That is one of the reasons for a newly added chapter to this edition. Chapter 8 contains eight faith-shaping experiences that make the Scriptures come to life in new and exciting ways.

Many of the materials available in youth ministry are based on the experiential education model. The goal is to set up a situation in which the class members or individuals can experience something for themselves or in which they can draw upon their life experiences. But the educational key is to debrief the experience afterward so that the participants are aware of what happened and what they gained.

In one church, a Sunday school teacher decided to prepare a lesson on how we prejudge others. The church had just finished redecorating the youth lounge where the class met. The class members took a lot of pride in the room. The teacher turned furniture over and scattered papers and pencils around as if someone had ransacked the room. The church had been broken into on several occasions, and the teacher was hoping that the class would jump to the conclusion that someone had broken in again.

What the teacher did not know was that another youth group had spent a night in the church during the weekend and had left a note thanking the group for letting them use the lounge. In the process of cleaning up the room, the note was discovered; and the class jumped to the conclusion that the visiting group had trashed the youth lounge. The class members were outraged and verbal in its anger toward the visiting group. Later, when the teacher explained what had really happened to the room, the class members were able to explore their own tendency to prejudge others.

## 6. Use Variety

Anything can get old. This statement is particularly true when working with teenagers. The word *boring* is their kiss of death for any activity or event. Variety is the best way to keep youth interested. They love to be surprised; they love the unexpected—especially true when approaching the Bible. Any Bible study method, even the most innovative and exciting, can be overused.

## 7. Provide Challenging, Depth Options

Often, curriculum and classes are set at a basic level. Many young people are offended if they sense that a class or study is aimed beneath them. If anything, it is better to shoot above the class members than to shoot below them. Youth love to be challenged. Many churches find that their middle school youth are ready for activities and resources that were supposedly for high school youth. And many churches have difficulty finding anything that can sufficiently challenge their high school youth.

To keep interest and to spur growth, we can seek more challenging curriculum and provide depth experiences of our own making. Some youth may not be willing to be involved in an in-depth Bible study, but others will be. If we are not sensitive to this need, we run the risk of losing the students who have the most potential in their spiritual growth.

*"It really means a lot to me to have a chance to study the Bible in depth. It seems like we have covered the same things in Sunday school for years but never really learn anything new. Last year, when we formed a new class to study the Bible in a deep way, I was excited. I like being able to learn new things and be involved in deep discussions."*

Eric, age 18

## 8. Use Groups and Group Dynamics

Most teenagers love to be in groups. Isolation and being alone are experienced as negative. When doing Bible study with adolescents, we need to be aware of this feeling and use it to our advantage. Group studies and group experiences are ideal. We need to be careful about techniques that involve solitude and depend on the individual's ability to work alone. We can use techniques that incorporate solitude, especially with those in senior high; but techniques that use the group will be our mainstay.

## 9. Use Discussion

One goal of most group Bible-study techniques is to stimulate discussion. Once an experience or activity has been done, the payoff is in the discussion that follows. Discussion is a mutual give-and-take in which young people get a chance to react to the ideas, opinions, and experiences of others and hear how others react to theirs. A good discussion forces individuals to hear and consider options they would not otherwise have considered.

Discussion is not teacher based but student based. The teacher simply guides classroom discussion. The teacher is not an expert who knows all and tells all. Rather, the teacher helps the class members process their own thoughts and insights. And at appropriate moments, the teacher can enter the discussion as a co-participant.

One of the driving paradigms in youth ministry today is that of small-group ministry. Chapter 5 offers some tips for that setting. Small groups are popular because in them youth can know and be known; youth can explore the faith in an intimate and personal setting. In the small-group setting, discussion is a crucial tool.

## 10. Allow for Direct Participation

Adolescents have a limited tolerance for sitting and listening to someone else do a presentation. The attention span of a teenager listening to an adult lecturer is shorter than the adult would think. In most settings, lecture is not a desirable way to approach Bible study with young people. Techniques that involve teenagers directly through leadership and participation keep the class's interest and enhance the learning experience. Members of the class can do much of the mechanics of the Bible study. They can read, write down what is said, lead activities, and lead discussions. In addition, they can be challenged to encounter the text directly and encouraged to form their own ideas and conclusions.

## *Know How to Ask the Right Questions*

Regardless of the technique used, knowing the right questions to ask during the debriefing strengthens Bible study. Three main areas need to be addressed through questions:

1. information (what the text actually says)
2. interpretation (what the text means)
3. application (what difference the text can make in our lives)

Students involved in Bible study need to understand what the passage says, what it means, and how they can apply it to their own lives.

## *Bible Study Techniques That Work With Youth*

There are hundreds of Bible study techniques. Many of these techniques are mentioned in the books listed in the bibliography. Below, you will find some techniques that are particularly suited for youth work.

## Guided Meditations on Scripture

The basic idea for this form of Bible study goes back to Ignatius of Loyola and has been around for hundreds of years. The leader guides the class through a meditation on a passage of Scripture and invites the class members to use their imagination to recreate the story and enter into it as participants. Instead of making the passage of Scripture an object to be examined and understood, the Scripture becomes a reality that the students enter into.

There are four key guidelines for doing an Ignatian meditation:

1. Place your class within the biblical scene. It is important for the person to place himself or herself within the story. This is done through imagination. As the leader guides the class through the story, the listeners are invited to imagine that they are present in the story.
2. Have the class members use their five physical senses to make the story come alive. I know a teacher who reads the text aloud five times, each time inviting the participants to use one of their senses. What would you see? What colors? Where is the light coming from? What would you smell? What textures would you feel? What would you hear? A simpler and more direct method is to stop several times at appropriate places during the story and ask the students what they see, hear, smell, feel, or taste.
3. Invite each class member to become a character in the story. As the story is read, the listener becomes a character in the story, not just an outside observer. In some cases, you may want to specify which characters the students are to play. In other cases, you may want to ask them to become characters but leave the decision as to which character up to them.
4. Talk about the passage as an experience that each class member went through. When the meditation is complete, the follow-up discussion needs to be based on what each person experienced as a participant in the story. What did you see? What emotions did you feel? What happened to you? What did Jesus say to you? How did you respond?

In addition to the four guidelines mentioned above, here are some practical suggestions that will help guided meditations go more smoothly and be more effective:

- Darken the room.
- If possible, have the class members lie on the floor.
- Instruct the students to close their eyes.
- Do the entire meditation in silence. Only the leader speaks.
- Use soft background music. The sound can help cover up distracting noises.
- Use breathing exercises like those mentioned in the example below to relax the class members.
- Allow periods of silence after each statement so that each person can use his or her imagination to experience that part of the text.

**Example: Ignatian Meditation on John 1:35-42 (Jesus calls his first disciples.)**
Briefly explain to the class what you will be doing. Challenge the participants by telling them that this experience can be extremely powerful and moving and that the more they put into the exercise, the more they will get out of it.

Have the youth spread out across the room and get comfortable. No one should be touching another person or close enough to disturb another. If possible, have the class members lie on the floor. Turn the lights out, and have the students close their eyes.

# Bible Study

If possible, play soft instrumental music in the background. Ask the students to take several slow, deep breaths. Then slowly read aloud the following meditation. Be sure to pause after each sentence (. . . .).

Imagine that you lived a long time ago in Israel. . . . You're standing with two friends outside a small town. . . . Look around. What do you see? . . . Feel the sun and the breeze on your skin. . . . What sounds do you hear? . . . One of your friends is John the Baptist. What does he look like? . . . You are standing there because you are waiting to see Jesus of Nazareth. What are you feeling as you wait? . . . In the distance, a man is walking toward you. . . . John becomes excited, points at the man, and says, "This is Jesus; this is the Lamb of God." Look at Jesus as he comes toward you. . . . What does he look like?. . . . What thoughts and feelings are you having? . . . As Jesus walks by, you begin to follow him. Why? . . . Jesus turns around, looks at you, and asks, "What do you want?" . . . After a few moments, you answer, "Teacher, where do you live?" Jesus answers: "Come and see." What is it that Jesus is going to show you? . . . You spend the afternoon with him. What do you do? . . . What do you talk about? . . . Jesus says something to you; it is. . . . You reply by saying. . . . You ask Jesus a question, something that you've always wanted to know. What do you ask? . . . His answer is. . . . Continue this conversation for a few moments. . . . How do you feel about being with him. . . . There is something about this man. You realize that in him you have found something you have been looking for. What is it? . . .
Have the class members open their eyes and form a circle. Debrief the experience by asking the following questions. Seek several responses to each question.

- What was that experience like for you?
- How does this experience differ from the way we usually study the Bible?
- How difficult was it to get into the story?
- What did you see or hear?
- What was your reaction to John the Baptist?
- How did you feel when Jesus first came up?
- What did Jesus took like?
- When Jesus asked you what you wanted, what did you answer?
- What did you talk about with Jesus?
- What feelings did you experience in Jesus' presence?

After the debriefing, have someone read aloud John 1:29-34. Ask the class members how the meditation changed the way they see that story.

Ignatian or guided meditation method of Bible study is particularly useful with stories or narratives. You can use the one above as a model for doing this approach with hundreds of stories in the Bible. In the Old Testament, you might want to use stories of youth or others who have encounters with God: the call of Samuel, the call of Jeremiah, Elijah's encounter with God at the mountain. In the New Testament, the Gospel stories and the Book of Acts are particularly helpful.

## Theological Bible Study

The basic idea behind this approach is to read the text and ask the following three questions, which Dr. Power says are central to any text:

- What does it say about God?
- What does it say about us as human beings?
- What does it say about the relationship between God and human beings?

For this approach, if the class is large, divide the class into three groups, each of which will read the passage and answer one of the questions. Then have the three groups report on what they discovered. Be sure that the youth don't get sidetracked by other issues, such as "Did it really happen?" or "How could it have happened?" The group is reading only for theological content: God, us, relationship.

Remember that the teacher not be the answer-giver but only one of many searchers. The source of information is the text itself, not the teacher.

### Example: Genesis 1:1–2:3 (The first story of Creation)

Begin by having someone read aloud the story. Explain the process that the youth will go through, and then divide the class into three groups (or repeat the three steps if the class is small). Assign each group one of the three topics. Give the groups several minutes to reread the passage and answer the questions. Make sure that each group has a facilitator who will keep the discussion going, a recorder who will keep notes, and a reporter who will make a verbal presentation to the whole class.

Have each of the groups make its report. Possible answers might include:

| God | Us | Relationship |
|---|---|---|
| powerful creator, source of everything, brings order out of disorder, creates good | creature, a part of creation, made in image of God, have responsibility for all of creation, good | We are dependent upon God. God put a lot of effort into creating us. |

As each group finishes its report, see if anyone else in the room can add anything on that topic. Repeat this process with the other two groups. When you are finished, ask:

- What have we learned about God from this passage?
- How does this fit what you already knew about God?
- What surprised you?

Repeat these three questions on the other two topics.

## Dialogue and Encounter

In this approach, several individuals or small groups work independently on a passage and then discuss what it means. The key is to push for alternative viewpoints rather than consensus. The power of this method lies in the likelihood that a collection of people, working independently, are more likely to encounter the richness of a text.

**Example: Isaiah 44:9-20 (Warning against idol worship)**

This passage is one that can be understood a lot of different ways. At a literal level, it is humorous, yet it quickly invites the reader to consider the idols we make for ourselves. By dividing the class into groups or giving several individuals the assignment of reading the passage on their own, you ensure a variety of opinions and observations. Allow time for each individual or group to read the passage. Have them be prepared to speak about the three major dimensions of meaning:

1. information (what it says)
2. interpretation (what it means)
3. application (what it means for us)

Expect a lively give-and-take at the third level.

## Paraphrase and Reverse Paraphrase

Paraphrase and reverse paraphrase are both delightful ways to make a text come alive. Both require students to use their own creativity. In paraphrase, the student or class rephrases the text in different language. Most often, the students are simply invited to put the text into their own words. However, this technique can be a lot more fun if it is done from a particular slant. Your youth know of groups in their schools or in society that have their own idiom or forms of expression. A text can be paraphrased from one of these perspectives: talk show host; sports announcer; pop music diva or rapper; cartoon character; game show host; old West character; professional wrestler—the possibilities are endless. Current TV shows or movies provide many possibilities.

If several different groups or individuals paraphrase the same text in a variety of ways, the results can be hilarious and also insightful.

Reverse paraphrase is paraphrasing but with a twist. In reverse paraphrase, the wording is reversed so that the meaning is exactly the opposite. This switch has a shock effect that forces the person to think about what the words really mean, as in this reverse paraphrase of a portion of Psalm 23:

The Lord is not my shepherd,
I have nothing.
I get no rest;
God tosses me about in a raging river.
and batters my spirit.
God guides me into evil.

Even when I walk in the midst of life,
I am terrified,
for God is against me.
I fear everything,
for I have been abandoned by God. . . .

Both of these approaches work well with passages that are so familiar that they have lost their effect. But they also work well with passages that are difficult to understand. Debrief the experience by asking the class members what new insights they gained from the exercise.

## Roleplay

Roleplays are another form of Bible study that work particularly well with stories, especially stories that have characters or issues with which teenagers can identify. In a roleplay, students take on the roles of characters and then act out the scenario in the passage. There are several ways to do this. One is to stick with the passage as if it were a script and simply have the class act out the scene as written. A twist on this approach is to have the actors place the story in a contemporary context.

Another approach is to have the class members assume the roles of the characters in the story and then go beyond what the text says and continue the story in a way they feel is faithful to the characters.

### Example: Genesis 37 (Joseph and his brothers)

A role play of this passage would include several main characters: Joseph, Israel (his father), a couple of brothers (or sisters), and his brother Reuben. Have the class study the story and the characters in the story. Make sure that any questions are answered. Then have volunteers take the roles of the characters and play out the story.

Afterward, ask each person what it was like to be the character he or she portrayed. What did this person think? feel? Why did this person behave the way he or she did? End by asking the class members what they learned about the story by doing the roleplay.

Another option is to interview the Bible figures from the roleplay and have them answer questions "in character," as they feel that their characters would answer the questions.

## Gestalt Roleplay

In a gestalt roleplay, one person plays two roles or or the two sides of one person. Chairs symbolize the roles. When a person is in one chair, he or she is one character. When the person moves to the other chair, the other character is present and speaking.

### Examples

This kind of roleplay can be done in several ways. One way is to involve two separate characters. For example, in Matthew 4:1-11 (the temptations of Jesus) one chair represents Jesus; the other chair represents the devil. The person doing the roleplay acts out the drama of the temptations by switching back and forth between the two chairs and the two characters. Afterward, the class members could interview the two characters as to why each said or did certain things.

Another approach is to let the two chairs represent two parts of the same person. In the case of Paul's inner struggle in Romans 7:14-25, one chair could represent the side of Paul that wants to be good, while the other chair represents the side of Paul that wants to be bad. Many teenagers would readily identify with a conversation between these two sides of Paul.

At a more complicated level, you could have several chairs, representing the various parts of the body described in 1 Corinthians 12:12-30. It would be easy to have a lively discussion among the various parts (hand, foot, eye, and ear). For a twist, the roleplay could be followed by a discussion in which the parts are renamed to fit a more contemporary and specific situation: youth group, older adults, parents, the church staff, nerds, jocks, socials, skaters, and so forth.

When the discussion is over, the various characters could be interviewed as to why they said or did certain things. This could lead into a discussion of issues that are relevant to the group—that is, why certain people feel unimportant or others seem to have an inflated sense of self, and what Paul's statements have to say about that situation.

## Devotional Reading

The basis of this approach is to read the Bible from the perspective of asking what it is that God has to say to the reader right now through this passage. Devotional reading assumes that the text is not just a historical document, but that—through the Holy Spirit—God can and does still speak through the Scripture. In this approach, the reader seeks not so much to understand as to hear and obey.

In using this approach, each individual must have time to read the text privately and to reflect on it. Afterward, bring the group together and have them talk about what they feel God is saying to each of them.

### Example: 1 Timothy 4:12 (Young people are important to God.)

Don, an eleventh grader, is active in church and is mature beyond his years. He has a lot to offer. Yet often, he does not feel that he is taken seriously by adults. He feels that his ideas and contributions are disregarded simply because he is not an adult. When Don read this passage, the first thing that stood out for him was that he should let no one disregard him because he is young. As Paul speaks this word of encouragement to Timothy, he speaks it to Don and to countless others. Don also remembered what Jesus said to his disciples, concerning children: "Let the little children come to me, and do not stop them; for it is to such as these that the kingdom of heaven belongs" (Matthew 19:14). What Don heard is that he is important to God that God takes him seriously even if others do not.

But as Don read on, he got a clearer idea of what he can actually do when he is not being taken seriously: "Set the believers an example in speech and conduct, in love, in faith, in purity." When Don read these words at summer camp, he heard God speaking to him, saying something he needed to hear. He was important in the eyes of God, and he wasn't the first person not taken seriously because he was young. Don also gained an insight into how he can be taken seriously: He can be an example, through his life, of what a Christian is called to be.

## Meditating on Scripture

Meditating on Scripture is similar to devotional reading, but it is freer. In meditation, a person reads a passage and then rereads it, looking for what stands out—a word, a phrase, an image, a thought provoked by what the text says. In meditation, the Scripture becomes the starting point. The person meditating on Scripture then begins to free-associate, or think about the word, phrase, or image to see where it may lead. The meditator is not limited by what the Scripture is saying.

**Example: Exodus 20:12 (Parental relationship)**

A junior high student may read a passage about honoring your father and mother, and the meditation may lead him or her into thinking about his or her relationship with a particular parent, the problems in that relationship, and what needs to be done to make the relationship more healthy.

## Journaling

Both devotional reading and meditation on Scripture can be done without journaling, but journaling enhances both. A journal is like a diary. The person writes down his or her thoughts, ideas, feelings, questions, and so on for further reflection. In Bible study, journaling becomes a means of gathering one's thoughts and feelings so that they can be expressed later. Journaling exercises can include letters to God (what you want to say to God), or letters from God (what you think God might say to you), or dialogues with God. Journaling may be as simple as a few words or sentences, or as complex as entries that go on for pages.

**Example**

In a Bible study, the group first reads a passage then spends time journaling thoughts and feelings. Afterward, the group comes back together and talks about what they have written. The more trust there is in a group, the more depth there can be to this exercise. Journaling works best in a weekend retreat setting or in an ongoing small group in which the members are committed to one another.

## Biblical Debate

In a biblical debate, participants debate two opposite sides of an issue, using the Scripture as a basis. No matter what the topic is—abortion, homosexuality, war—the approach is the same. Each side in the debate attempts to be faithful to the Scripture, to see how what it has to say sheds light on the topic.

**Example: Abortion**

These debates usually follow a semi-formal format. Divide the class into two groups and assign their positions. One will be pro-choice; the other will be pro-life. Give both groups Scripture references that could be used by their side. Tell them that their assignment will be to argue from a Christian perspective, using the biblical passages you have given them (and any others they can think of) as resources. Give the two groups time to do research and to prepare their arguments.

Then have each side present its argument. Give both sides the same amount of time. Then give both sides a few minutes to prepare their rebuttals. Each side then has a few minutes to argue against what the opposing team has presented. After this is done, tell the class that in a Bible study, it is not important to have one side win and one side lose. Instead, after the debate, move the class into a discussion of what they learned about the topic.

A twist on this approach is to find out which side of an issue the members of the class agree with and have them take the opposite view. Those who were pro-life would take the pro-choice position and vice versa. This switch forces the class members to consider the other side of a an issue. This does not mean they must agree with the other position. But it will help them understand it better.

*"I remember the time we were studying abortion in our evening youth group. We decided to research the topic and have a debate. We split up into two groups: one group for abortion and the other against it. Then the sponsors made all those who were against abortion research the pro-choice position from a Christian viewpoint, and then argue for it. The pro-choice group did the same with the pro-life view. It really made me think about the issue in new ways. It didn't change my beliefs, but it made me realize that it is more complicated than I had thought."*

Jana, age 13

## Spectrum Bible Study

The idea behind spectrum Bible study is to get as many different interpretations of a passage as possible, and then see what those collective interpretations tell us about the passage. But rather than the interpretations being each person's private opinion of what the text says, as in dialogue and encounter, the class looks at the passage from a variety of pre-determined positions. Spectrum Bible study uses four of these approaches: literal, allegorical, spiritually true, only a story.

### Example: Matthew 13:4-9, 18-23 (Parable of the Sower)

For spectrum Bible study, divide the class into four groups and assign each group one of the four approaches. If the group is small, do the four steps sequentially. The literal group reads the passage from the perspective of taking every single word at its literal meaning. The allegorical group assumes that everything in the text means something else. (An example of this approach is found in the Gospel of Matthew. In Matthew 13:4-9, Jesus tells the parable of the sower. A few verses later, in Matthew 13:18-23, the parable is explained as an allegory. Everything symbolizes something else. All the types of seed and soil become types of people.) The spiritually true group looks for the religious truth in the passage—what it says about God and the things of God. The story group looks at the passage as only a story.

Each group reports its findings, based on its own approach. Then the whole class discusses the following four questions:

- What is each point of view actually saying?
- What value does each position attempt to uphold?
- What are some problems with each view?
- What are some implications of each view?

Finally, ask the youth what they learned about the passage through this approach.

## Exploring Personal Problems Through Bible Study

People have always used the Scriptures to deal with personal problems and issues. As a particular form of Bible study, this approach begins with a personal issue and then moves to the Scriptures as a resource. The group will begin by focusing on a common problem, issue, or experience, and then bring selected passages of Scripture to bear on the issue to see what light they shed.

The procedure has three steps:

1. a time of dealing with the personal problem
2. a time devoted to looking at selected Scriptures (a Bible that has Scripture referenced to key topics can be a valuable tool)
3. a discussion period in which there is dialogue between the problem and the Scriptures

This approach lends itself naturally to adolescents and is the model behind a lot of contemporary curriculum.

### Example: Romans 7:14-25 (Paul's inner struggle)

Begin by involving the class in a discussion of times when they have not understood their own behavior. Model what you are asking for by telling of a time when you either did something that you knew was wrong or did not do something that you knew was right. Have several others talk about their experiences.

Ask: "Why do we do this?" Involve the class in a discussion that focuses on what it is like to want to do one thing but to do another. Then have someone read aloud Romans 7:14-25 and see whether the class members can identify with Paul's feelings. You may supplement this passage with some stories from the Scriptures that illustrate this human tendency—for instance, the story of David and Bathsheba (2 Samuel) or Jesus in the garden of Gethsemane (Matthew 26).

Have a member of the class read aloud verse 24. Ask the following questions:

• What is Paul talking about?
• How does God make a difference when we think that we can't do what is right?

Finish the Bible study by focusing on how God's love and forgiveness can make a difference when we feel as if we cannot handle something ourselves.

## Relational Bible Study

This approach to Bible study is similar to the theological one, in that it focuses on particular aspects of a Bible text. In this approach, however, the focus is on relationships. The text is read for what it has to say about relationships. The focus is on these four levels of relationship:

1. our relationship with God
2. our relationship with ourselves
3. our relationship with other people
4. our relationship to the world

The key to relational Bible study is not to get sidetracked into data or detail but to remain focused on the relational nature of the Bible. We may not understand relationships at a rational level. And we don't understand a lot about relationships, due to the changes in culture and world view over the centuries. But the basic qualities of relationships remain unchanged over the ages. Human beings still struggle with the same relational issues that they did three thousand years ago: love, passion, greed, lust, alienation, jealousy, anger, joy. In the stories of the Bible, we see our relationships and ourselves.

### Example: Psalm 8 (The majesty of God)

Read aloud the psalm. Answer any questions the class members have about this passage. Then divide the class into four study groups. Assign each group one of the four dimensions of relationship. Tell the groups that all four dimensions are in the psalm, but some dimensions will be easier to spot than others. Give the groups time to read the passage and identify the aspects of relationship for which they are looking.

Bring the groups back together and have each group report its findings. After each report is given, involve the class in a discussion of what the passage is saying and what it has to say to us today. End by asking the following:

- How does looking at the relationships in this passage help us understand the passage?
- How does it help us understand ourselves better?

## Affective Bible Study

Often in Bible study, we focus on the cognitive content of the passage. For some texts that may be adequate, but for many it will be inadequate. The Bible is a story of people and relationships. It brims with emotion. To ignore the emotional or affective content of the Bible is to drain it of much of its power.

Affective Bible study focuses on the emotional content of a passage to discover what the feelings expressed can say to us. This approach is especially appropriate for the Psalms or for narrative stories. But it can be used with almost any text, including a highly theological text like the one in the example below. Affective Bible study has four steps:

1. The passage is read with attention to the emotions present or expressed.
2. Two questions are asked to help the class deal with the emotional content:
   - What feelings are present?
   - Why, do you think, does the author or the character in the story feel this way?
3. There is a time of personal sharing, facilitated by two questions that connect the passage to the life of the group:
   - Have you ever felt this way? When? Where? (Encourage the students to narrate a story from their own lives that parallels the one in the passage.)
   - Is anyone experiencing this right now?
4. Through two questions, seek guidance from the passage in dealing with the personal issues expressed:
   - Did the writer or character in the story experience any resolution with the issue presented there?
   - Is there anything we can learn from the Bible passage that can help us with our issue?

**Example: Galatians 3:1-5 (Law or faith)**

Have the group begin by reading the passage. Use the first two questions to help the group identify the feelings present and why Paul feels so strongly. Since this is a theological passage and the portion being studied is part of a larger section (Chapters 3–4), you may want to read the longer passage and be prepared to give a brief explanation of what is behind Paul's anger. You could say something like, "Paul has discovered that some of the people in the church at Galatia who had accepted Jesus and become Christians have now abandoned everything they were taught and have returned to their earlier religion."

Do not focus on what happened there in Galatia two thousand years ago. Rather, you want to use the issue and Paul's anger to evoke similar experiences or feelings within the class.

Once you think that the youth have a basic understanding of the text, move to the third step. Have the class members identify times when they have felt angry or betrayed by others. Invite volunteers to tell their own stories to the class.

Reserve some time to move to the fourth and final step. Can the youth see anything in the way Paul dealt with his anger that would be helpful to them? If the students can't find anything in the passage as read, invite them to read on for several more verses.

## Transformational (Behavioral) Bible Study

Transformational Bible study focuses on how the Bible can motivate and enable behavioral change. This approach takes seriously the biblical mandate to be transformed into the image of the invisible God. In theological terms, transformational Bible study sees the Scripture as a resource for the ongoing process of Christian formation—growth in holiness. Transformational Bible study uses four key questions:

- What truth does this passage teach? (What should we believe?)
- How does the passage reveal and rebuke error? (What should we reject?)
- What can be learned from this passage to help correct faults and put things right? (How can we change?)
- What instructions does this passage give to direct our daily living? (How should we behave?)

**Example: 2 Timothy 3:14-17 (Scripture equips us for good work.)**

This passage is ideal as an introduction to transformational Bible study, since it argues for the transformational nature of Scripture itself. Have the class read the passage, and then give everyone a few moments to make notes and write down any questions that come to mind. Ask the first question above and invite the group members to give their responses. Encourage discussion and group interaction. Repeat the process with the other three questions.

End by asking: "What do we need to do this week to put this passage into practice?" Allow plenty of time for this step, as it is the heart of transformational Bible study. Encourage each person present to struggle with the question and form his or her own individual response. Have each person tell what he or she needs to do. End with a prayer in which you ask for God's strength and guidance.

## Dialogue With Contemporary Life

This approach seeks to take something from contemporary life to raise an issue, and then bring the Scripture into a dialogue with that item. It is helpful if something from contemporary life has captured the attention of the group, whether it is a news item, a song, or something from a movie or TV.

### Example: Current Events, Music, or Other Media

In the case of current events, the newspaper, newsmagazines, or television news can be used as a resource. If the local newspaper reports a change in policy by the school board on locker searches at the high school, there will he a high level of interest in this topic. This article could be used as a springboard to explore the right to privacy versus the right to safety for the school and its students. A variety of passages could be used for this purpose.

A popular song on the radio or a video on TV could be used to raise a faith or moral issue. Years ago, the rock group Depeche Mode had a song called "Policy of Truth." The song begins with a recording of Richard Nixon's voice, saying, "I want to tell my side of the story," then goes on to reflect on the nature of truth and lying. The relevance of this topic for the Christian community is obvious. But by starting with the song, a group might be more motivated to discuss the topic. Few youth today will have ever heard of that song, but use contemporary songs that raise similar topics. In addition, the emergence of contemporary Christian music as a major force in our society provides a whole new source for music and lyrics.

Other media also provide opportunities to find material: movie releases, television shows, articles from magazines. Many of these raise and deal with important faith issues and issues of concern to youth. The basic format for this approach would be the same no matter what the resource.

- Use the resource to raise the issue.
- Hand out the newspaper article, play the song, show the video, and so forth.
- Have the group discuss the resource and see what issues it raises for them.
- Have the class read one or more passages of Scripture that deal with that issue or are relevant to the issue.
- Have the class carry on a dialogue between the issue raised and the Scripture resource.
- Have the group summarize how the Scripture might help in dealing with the issue.

## Depth and Encounter

This study method combines several of the methods mentioned above for a more powerful effect. It combines paraphrase, depth Bible study, and transformational Bible study.

### Example: Galatians 5:13-26 (Called to freedom)

Begin by having the class read and paraphrase a portion of this passage, verse by verse. You may want to select a portion of the text for the whole class or divide the passage into smaller parts and assign it to different groups or individuals.

Then ask the class to consider what would happen if this passage and what it is saying were taken seriously. How would their lives change? If the class is large, divide the youth into small groups and have them talk about their answers to this question.

Finally, reassemble the class and have volunteers tell what was discussed in each group. Ask: "What challenges or impresses you most deeply from this passage or from the discussion?"

## Movement

The beginning of this chapter contained several examples of exciting, innovative ways to study the Bible. One of these uses movement. Use movement to express or encounter what the text is talking about. One activity that deals with the issue of brokenness and reconciliation has youth breaking physical contact, walking away, turning around, closing their eyes—all to symbolize and act out the brokenness of our world. Walking back toward the group, turning back toward the group, reestablishing physical contact, and opening eyes—each of these symbolizes reconciliation. Trust exercises, in which people are passed around physically or caught when they drop, become a way of experiencing faith through their body. Printed curriculum resources are filled with activities like these; and once you have done a few of them, you can easily create your own.

## DISCIPLE Bible Study for Youth

This chapter has been devoted to Bible study techniques, not to prepackaged Bible study programs, of which there are many: Bethel, Trinity, Kerygma, and so on. DISCIPLE Bible study is listed here for two reasons: (1) because it is a uniquely powerful approach to Bible study that focuses not just on biblical knowledge but on responding to God's call to discipleship. It also uses many of the techniques and ideas advocated in this chapter—small groups, experiential learning, discussion, and so on. And (2) the youth edition of DISCIPLE: *BECOMING DISCIPLES THROUGH BIBLE STUDY* is specifically designed to be used by youth.

DISCIPLE is a systematic survey of the Bible that lasts for nine months. It is not exhaustive, in the sense that every verse in the Bible is read. Rather, it is comprehensive, in the sense that major portions of most books are read and the basic themes of the Bible are covered.

In the DISCIPLE program, a small group (12 or so) of young people in 10th grade or older covenant with the group leader to spend nine months together, reading the Bible from the perspective of spiritual growth. The main question behind the whole package is "How can I become a more faithful disciple?"

DISCIPLE has two key elements: daily home readings of Scriptures and a two-hour, weekly group session. Each student has a study manual that gives assignments and additional resources. The students read and make notes for six days and rest on the seventh. The readings also include questions that are personal rather than academic and a section on "The Marks of Discipleship," in which each person is invited to respond to the call of discipleship in a personal way.

The group sessions begin with a brief time of personal concerns and prayers. Then a brief video segment is shown. One of the unique qualities of DISCIPLE is that each week, through the videotape, the class has access to an outstanding biblical scholar and teacher. The tape is then discussed, and the group moves into a day-by-day discussion of the Scripture readings and participants' comments and questions. Then the class will do an experiential Bible study. The teacher helps suggests a variety of approaches, including several of those in this chapter. The group session ends with personal sharing based on "The Marks of Discipleship."

DISCIPLE is different from many other forms of youth Bible study, in that the adult leading the group is not a teacher in the traditional sense. Instead, the adult functions as a group facilitator. The information does not flow from the teacher to the group. It flows from the Bible to the group members and from the group members to one another. One of the reasons for the required training of DISCIPLE teachers is to help them understand that they are not to "teach" in the traditional way.

DISCIPLE has two major challenges. The first is financial. With the study manuals, videotapes, and required training, it is expensive. The cost is in the hundreds of dollars. Many groups invite participants to share the cost by paying for their own study manual. The second challenge is in the area of commitment. DISCIPLE involves a major commitment of time and effort on the part of those who take it. It is not for everyone.

Counterbalancing these two challenges is my personal conviction that the youth edition of DISCIPLE: BECOMING DISCIPLES THROUGH BIBLE STUDY is the single most powerful tool currently available for serious study of the Scriptures with youth. It works. It does things that nothing else can.

For more information about DISCIPLE Bible study, call toll-free 800-251-8591 or 800-672-1789, or write to DISCIPLE, P.O. Box 801, 201 Eighth Avenue, South, Nashville TN 37202-0801.

## Other Sources

Curriculum resources specialize in Bible studies. Some are Bible to life; others are life to Bible. The methods to engage youth are wide ranging and often extra creative. As with any resource, you will want to make it your own, make it fit your group and their needs. However, the written resources provide excellent starting places and a broader range of ideas than you might think of on your own. Check with your denominational publishing house for more information about what is available.

With the advent of the World Wide Web, new avenues for finding and creating Bible studies are at our fingertips. One Web site in particular to check out is *www.ileadyouth.com*. It is a searchable database of resources, some of which are downloadable; others are available as printed volumes.

In addition, this particular site has two other major benefits:

1. Its search capability. Simply type in a Scripture passage or book and site gives you a listing with annotations of the various sessions built around your choice of biblical material.

2. Its infinite growth. Every quarter new materials are added to the site. Currently, the database has nearly 500 topics. Watch the numbers climb.

# CHAPTER 2

# PRAYER: SPEAKING TO GOD

**K**elly was leading the prayer time during our regular evening youth fellowship. As members of the youth group shared joys, concerns, and prayer requests, Kelly led the group in the response, "Hear our prayer, O Lord." Then she gave one of the most eloquent prayers I have ever heard. The prayer was from her heart and spoke directly to the concerns that had been expressed. Everyone was moved.

As Kelly prayed, my mind flashed back to an evening two years before, the first time I had asked her to pray in front of the group. Her answer had been immediate and emphatic: "I can't pray!"

I then asked, "Can you say, 'Dear God, thank you for everything. Amen'?" She gave me a funny look and answered, "Sure, I can do that!" So I asked her to do it. And she did. Afterward, she looked up at me with a smile and beamed with a look of accomplishment.

Kelly's problem wasn't that she couldn't pray. She could and she did. Her problem was that two things stood in the way of her praying. The first was her understanding of prayer. She associated prayer with what she had seen pastors and other adults do. Her mental image was of long, elaborate prayers that seemed to go on and on and mentioned everything under the sun. Kelly was convinced that she couldn't do that. She was not aware that a prayer could be short and simple.

The second problem Kelly faced in praying was that no one had ever taught her how to pray. Others had always prayed for her. She never had the opportunity to practice and develop this skill, for prayer is a skill. Prayer is learned, and whatever can be learned can be taught.

## *Jesus Teaches His Disciples How to Pray*

In an interesting story in the eleventh chapter of Luke, the disciples of Jesus ask him to teach them how to pray. We are familiar with this passage because it contains the Lord's Prayer, which follows; but the situation itself is worth looking at:

**Luke 11:1-4**

[1] [Jesus] was praying in a certain place, and after he had finished, one of his disciples said to him, "Lord, teach us to pray, as John taught his disciples." [2] He said to them, "When you pray, say:

Father, hallowed be your name.
　Your kingdom come.
　[3] Give us each day our daily bread.
　[4] And forgive us our sins,
　　for we ourselves forgive everyone indebted to us.
　And do not put us to the time of trial."

For those of us who work with young people and want to help them develop a personal spiritual life, several things are interesting about this passage. First, what provoked the request to be taught was that Jesus himself was praying and the disciples had observed him. Jesus modeled prayer in his own life, and this modeling had an effect on the disciples. They wanted to learn how to do what Jesus was doing.

Second, the disciples acknowledged that they did not know how to pray. Prayer was not a skill they were born with but one they needed to develop. Like Kelly, they needed to be taught.

Third, they had apparently seen Jesus' cousin John teaching his disciples to pray. They wanted Jesus to do what they had already seen John doing—giving instruction on a specific skill: how to pray.

Fourth, what stands out is the Lord's Prayer itself, which Jesus puts forward as a model. In stark contrast with much of the prayer we have in the world today, Jesus' prayer is a model of simplicity. With few words, it speaks directly to the basic issues of life. In the version of the Lord's Prayer found in the Gospel of Matthew, Jesus specifically warns the disciples against praying in ways that are pretentious:

**Matthew 6:7-8**

[7] "When you are praying, do not heap up empty phrases as the Gentiles do; for they think that they will be heard because of their many words. [8] Do not be like them, for your Father knows what you need before you ask him."

Prayer is a skill; it is learned. This means that prayer can be taught. We need only to remove unnecessary obstacles to prayer and give the youth we work with opportunities to develop this important skill. This and the following chapter will help you think through your own understanding of prayer, give you some guidelines for working with youth, and give you numerous tried-and-true techniques that you can use with your group.

People are different. Researchers have noted, for example, that different people have different styles of learning. Some are visual/spatial learners. Others are verbal/linguistic learners. Still others are interpersonal, or intrapersonal, or logical/mathematical, or body/kinesthetic, or musical/rhythmic learners. You can't expect all people to learn in the same way. What works for one person may not work for another.

In the same way, different people find different prayer techniques work better for them than do others. Several years ago I took a yearlong course on meditation and contemplation. One of the things I discovered was that this type of prayer did not come naturally to me. Yet other prayer forms do and speak deeply to me. Expect the same to be true about the youth with whom you work. One of the reasons for so many different prayer forms is that there are so many different kinds of people.

## *What Is Prayer?*

One of the obstacles we need to remove is the common confusion about what prayer is and is not. Almost anything can and has been said in the name of God in prayer. Abuses of prayer abound, both outside and within the church. It's little wonder that many young people are either confused about prayer or turned off by it. Recently I listened as two of our junior high students were parodying a popular televangelist praying. What they had accurately picked up on was a grotesquely distorted understanding of prayer. They were quite good. They had the fake intonation down pat. They knew how to say "Je-sus" with just the right effect. And they knew how to make outlandish requests for wealth and material possessions of God. But did they know how to pray?

Several centuries ago, the Protestant reformer Martin Luther made a couple of interesting observations about prayer that are still helpful today. Both of his observations are in the form of what prayer is not.

- First, prayer is not telling God something that God otherwise would not know. When we pray, we are not bringing God up to date on what is going on. As Jesus commented to his disciples, God knows our needs even before we speak (Matthew 6:8). Prayer does not *tell* God anything.
- Second, prayer is not a means of forcing God to do something that God would not otherwise do. Prayer is not leverage on God or a way to manipulate God. What God does, God does because of who God is, because of God's gracious nature. Prayer does not make God *do* anything.

That commentary raises an interesting question. If prayer is not telling God anything that God would not otherwise know or talking God into doing something that God would not otherwise do, then what is prayer? It's clear that if Martin Luther is correct, then we have eliminated much of what usually passes for prayer.

Martin Luther's point is that prayer is not for God at all. Prayer is for us. We don't pray because of the effect it has on God. We pray because of the effect it has on us. Prayer is a tool that God has given us for our own benefit. Prayer does not change God. It changes us and helps us.

But what is even more important is that prayer is the stuff of relationship. Prayer is about communication, about talking to God and listening to God. Prayer is a tool that God has given us so that we can develop a personal relationship with God. The Christian faith is profoundly relational.

Spiritual growth has to do with developing our relationship with God. Prayer is conversation. It is talking to God and listening to God. Prayer makes us aware of who we are, of who God is, of what we need, and from whom we get what we need. Through prayer—in all of its many forms—we enter into communion and conversation with God.

Historically, the Christian faith has emphasized two major forms of prayer: active prayer (talking to God) and passive or dispositional prayer (listening to God). Like Bible study, prayer lies at the center of our faith. We grow in our faith as we develop our relationship with God. Common sense dictates that a relationship—any relationship—requires nurture and communication. Not only that, but it requires regular, ongoing communication. Any relationship can drift and deteriorate if it is not continually nurtured.

Relationships also require two-way communication. We need to learn how to speak to God, to open up our hearts and express our needs and desires; but we also need to learn how to listen to God. This chapter will focus on techniques for active prayer, or talking to God. The next chapter will cover techniques for dispositional prayer, or how to listen to God.

## *Guidelines for Teaching Youth to Pray*

As was the case with Bible study, prayer is much more than just mechanics. Because it is profoundly relational, what you are trying to teach is not so much mechanics as how to nurture and develop a relationship. In using any of the ideas that follow, a few simple guidelines will help:

### 1. Model Prayer

Youth learn more by what they see us do than by what they hear us say. One of the most effective tools we have in teaching adolescents how to pray is our own ability to pray. We are all, whether we like it or not, role models. And our ability to model not only how to pray but the importance of prayer in our own relationship with God also is crucial for teenagers. Jesus' disciples saw that prayer was important to Jesus, because they saw him praying. Our youth can learn the same thing from us.

### 2. Practice Prayer

The best way to learn how to pray is to pray. Anyone who has ever tried to learn a new skill knows the secret: practice, practice, practice. Studying prayer or talking about prayer can take us only so far. Like the now famous Nike commercial from several years ago, there comes a point when we "just do it."

Not only do we need to be praying, but we also need to make sure that the youth are praying. The more they pray, the more meaningful prayer will be to them and the more prayer will become integrated into their lives.

## 3. Provide Opportunities to Pray

If the teens are to practice prayer, then we need to find opportunities for them to pray. Every meeting can open and close with prayer. We can pray about concerns. We can use every available opportunity to lift feelings, concerns, issues, and thanksgiving to God in prayer.

## 4. Require Prayer

Prayer should not be an option. When we gather, we pray. When we depart, we pray. When we worship, we pray. When we have pains and sorrows, we pray. When we have joys, we pray. The practice of prayer comes first. An appreciation for prayer will follow. It is a mistake to ask a group if they want to pray. Prayer is a given. As Christians, we are a people who pray.

We need much in life that we may not want at a particular moment. Prayer is too important to be left to a vote or to our fickle feelings. John Wesley, the founder of the Methodist movement, once made the comment that we should "preach faith until we have it, and then when we have it, preach faith." In much the same way, we should pray until we develop an appreciation for prayer. Then, when we have an appreciation for it, we should pray.

## 5. Call On Youth to Pray

A certain amount of awkwardness and discomfort accompanies learning how to pray in front of others. It is not easy. Several years ago I was shocked by the practice of another youth minister, who would routinely, and without warning, call on a youth to pray. He would simply say, "Jim, pray for us." And Jim would. Jim was uncomfortable. Jim stumbled over his thoughts and his words. But he prayed. And, like Kelly, through his stumbling and awkwardness, Jim learned how to pray. But what is just as important, Jim was learning to pray aloud in a warm, supportive environment. Jim knew that he was not being asked to do anything that others would not also be asked to do later. And he knew that no one would make fun of him, no matter how awkward his attempts. Support and encouragement surrounded him.

There is nothing wrong with calling on youth to pray. The young person may feel uncomfortable, but the act of praying itself is the only way to overcome that discomfort. We need to provide the opportunities to pray and to make sure that the environment is safe and affirming.

## 6. Use Techniques That Involve Everyone

Many of the techniques that follow in this chapter allow a number of people to be involved in a prayer, rather than focusing on one person. Prayer forms, such as circle prayer, that involve everyone in the group make it easier for those who are uncomfortable with prayer to practice and become more comfortable.

## 7. Use Silence

Sometimes it is helpful to ask for a volunteer, rather than designating a particular person to pray. When you do this, allow plenty of time for silence. Most adolescents are more uncomfortable with silence than they are with prayer. If you ask for a volunteer and then allow for an extended period of silence, someone will usually offer to pray in order to end the silence.

## 8. Teach an Attitude of Prayer

Several years ago I worked with a volunteer who taught me to appreciate what she called "an attitude of prayer." What she meant by this was a tone or a mood. She taught our group that when we were in an attitude of prayer, there was to be a definite shift from what we had been doing. An attitude of prayer included becoming quiet, focusing on what we were doing, and using a tone of reverence. When someone said, "Let us pray," there was a perceptible change in the room. She taught me that youth can easily learn this attitude and come to value it highly. Once an attitude of prayer has been taught, the youth themselves become the ones who enforce it.

*"Every year, when the new seventh graders come into our youth group, I get so mad because they do not have an attitude of prayer. Being able to voice my prayer concerns in youth worship, hear the prayer requests of others, and take time at the altar to pray are important to me. I really miss it if I don't get a chance to pray each week."*

Stacey, age 14

## 9. Communicate Expectations

I have often heard the complaint that teenagers, especially those in middle school or junior high, are incapable of taking prayer or worship seriously They won't sit still. They talk during the prayer. They won't focus on what is going on. My own experience is exactly the opposite. I think that one of the issues here is a failure to communicate expectations. As a general rule of thumb, the more I expect, the more the youth come through. When I have problems, it is usually because I have failed to communicate what I expect.

Young people don't know what is expected until we tell them. They don't know what to do or to avoid until we clearly communicate our expectations. And teenagers need to be continually reminded. There will always be a learning curve. Few people get it right the first time they show up. But they learn. And our role is to teach them what is expected, to show them.

We cannot tell them what is expected and then assume that one teaching to do the job. We need to repeat ourselves again and again.

## 10. Deal With Disruptions

A lot of disruptions can be avoided by taking preventative measures. When we clearly communicate expectations, teach an attitude of prayer, have enough adults present, and use our relationships with the youth, many potential disruptions never arise. But teens are teens. They will make mistakes. They won't think.

When disruptions arise, three guidelines are helpful. First, confront the issues directly and immediately. A problem will rarely get better if it is ignored. Be honest. Tell the group what is bothering you. Don't use names or point out any particular person. Tell the group as a whole your concern about the disruption.

Second, use the group members. Ask the participants how they feels about what is going on. In many instances, the group is just as bothered—if not more so—than you are.

Third, after the event, if you have to, speak to the person who was disruptive. Never hold this conversation in front of others; doing so makes you the heavy and that youth the hero to his or her peers. Deal with the problem one on one. Tell the young person what bothers you, what you want; and then ask him or her to help you. Often disruptive behavior is an attention-getting technique. Give those who are disruptive the attention, but give it in a positive way.

## 11. Allow the Youth to Determine the Content of Their Own Prayers

Several years ago, one of the volunteers on our team came to me, upset by a prayer that was led by a junior high girl in worship. The group had been in a time of prayer. Those present were invited to lift their concerns to God. Several people in the group had revealed significant concerns: divorce, death, illness, broken relationships. Then one 7th grade girl prayed for her dog that had just died. The volunteer felt that this prayer was inappropriate, that it destroyed the serious mood of the prayer time because a couple of senior highs had laughed.

As it turned out, this was the girl's first experience with death; and the dog had been in the family as long as she had. The dog was more than a pet. It was a lifelong friend whom she had lost and for whom she grieved. She had lifted to God in the prayer this very deep and sincere pain. Her prayer over her dog's death was more than appropriate; it was critical to who she was as a child of God at that moment. Nothing could have been more genuine and powerful than her raising her pain and grief to God at this time of loss. We need to be extremely careful when we label something appropriate or inappropriate.

## 12. Provide an Environment of Prayer

Prayer works best when it is like the air we breathe. Prayer should not be sporadic, occasional, or alien. It should always be present, woven into the fabric of all we do. It should be a natural part of every activity. The more we weave prayer into our various activities and events, the more natural prayer will seem to the young people with whom we work.

## 13. Allow Time for Prayer to Develop

Prayer is a spiritual discipline. It is a skill. Skills and discipline are not learned overnight. First we learn to crawl. Then we learn to toddle, then walk, then run. Developing the prayer life of individual youth or of a group takes time and patience. We can't rush the results. We can only encourage and nurture the practice. And ultimately, we must trust the young people with whom we work and trust that God is at work in their lives.

## *Active Prayer Techniques That Work With Youth*

Most of the time, the praying we do involves what is called active prayer, or speaking to God. Active prayer involves addressing God with our concerns, our needs, and our agendas. In active prayer, we do the speaking, not because God needs the information, but because we need to share what is significant in our lives with the One who gave us life and who sustains us. Listed below you will find twenty-four ways you can use active prayer with youth groups.

## 1. Sandwich Prayer

A sandwich prayer is simply prayer that is used in opening and closing an activity. Like the bread on a sandwich, it covers both sides. It makes the statement that what we are doing is done in God's name and in God's presence. Anyone can do the praying, and it can have any content. Prayer becomes the bracket around the activity.

## 2. Circle Prayer

In a circle prayer, the group forms a circle; and each person around the circle, in turn, adds to the prayer. You can use any one of several techniques listed below: word, sentence completion, and so on. You may want to give individuals the option of passing. One way you can do this is to have the person who wants to pass squeeze the hand of the next person. The prayer then skips on to the next person. There is also an advantage to requiring each person to pray. The key is to strike a balance between gentle and loving pressure to pray (and, thereby, grow), and permission to pass.

Another option is to let a person raise what is called "an unspoken prayer." This allows the person to lift a prayer concern without having to say what the content of that concern is. The group may not know that the person raising the unspoken concern has a mother who has just been diagnosed with cancer. Allowing the person to lift an unspoken concern in the circle prayer makes it possible for the person to offer a genuine prayer concern without having to reveal something that he or she is not ready to acknowledge publicly.

## 3. Word Prayers

Word prayers are limited to a word or a short phrase. In this form of prayer, each person thanks God for something or asks God for something; but the prayer is limited to a word or phrase. The leader sets up and models the form, then each teen adds a word. The leader might say that we all thank God for one thing. Then the responses might include the following: parents, friends, this group. This format is less intimidating for young people who are afraid of prayer.

## 4. Sentence Prayers

Sentence prayers are extended word prayers. In these prayers, the participants are limited to one sentence, usually a short one. This can be done in a circle prayer format, or responsively, as in prayers or concerns.

## 5. Open-Ended Prayers

These are sometimes called sentence-completion prayers, a special form of sentence prayers in which the leader sets up the topic and the group members fill in the blank. Examples include: "Lord, I thank you for . . . ," "Lord, help me with . . . ," "God, I'm sorry that . . . ."

## 6. Build-a-Prayer Prayer

This special form of circle prayer is a lot of fun. One person begins the prayer and leaves it open-ended, as in "God, today we thank you for. . . ." The next person in the circle will pick up where the last person left off and continue but also leave it open-ended. The prayer continues around the circle until the last person adds a part and ends by saying, "Amen." This form of prayer can become frivolous; but it also can be a powerful and effective form of prayer, as each person literally builds on the prayer of the person before. A prayer might look like this: "Dear God, I pray that we . . . uh, are thankful for all you have given us, such as . . . our friends, . . . our parents, and. . . .

## 7. Responsive Prayer

This is sometimes called a "say-with-me prayer." It's like a responsive reading, except that the group members will repeat whatever the leader says. Any prayer can be done this way. If we were to do the Lord's Prayer (Matthew 6:9-13) as a responsive prayer, it would be done like this: "Our Father in heaven (Our Father in heaven), hallowed be your name (hallowed be your name), and so on.

## 8. Popcorn Prayers

In a popcorn prayer, various members of the group, wherever they are, stand up one at a time to give a prayer then sit down. There is no pattern to this. It is like kernels of popcorn that randomly pop up then go back down. The content of the prayer can vary. Group members can tell concerns, joys, or whatever.

In one form of this prayer, short statements can be written on sheets of paper and then distributed to participants to be read. The act of standing allows one person to be the focus of the prayer at that moment, gives the group a point to focus on, and helps the speaker be heard.

## 9. Waiting On the Lord Prayer

This form of prayer takes its name from the Quaker tradition of "waiting on the Lord." In this prayer form, the group enters into a time of silent prayer. Before the prayer begins, group members are invited to say prayers as the Spirit leads. During the time of silence, participants may lift up prayers as they feel led. Sometimes no one prays aloud. At other times, a few people will pray. Occasionally, a large number will pray. The prayer ends after a prolonged silence indicates that all who wish to contribute to the prayer have done so. The key to this form of prayer is that we should not be afraid of an extended silence at the beginning of the prayer.

## 10. Written Prayer

Group members can read prayers that are written. They may get these from books, or they may write the prayers themselves. Written prayers are most effective when they are short—anything much beyond 15 to 30 seconds can get boring. Written prayers are especially effective with those who are afraid of praying. Having the prayer written down and in their hands helps them deal with their anxiety.

## 11. Song Prayer

Many songs have lyrics that are prayers. These may be read like written prayers, or they may be sung. The Wesleyan Grace and Doxology are examples that many of us use. Group members may use songs from the hymnal, songs from contemporary songbooks, or songs from contemporary Christian artists. We are especially blessed today with a wealth of short praise songs and choruses that are essentially prayers.

## 12. Silent Prayer

Silence allows group members to express their concerns in ways that they might not verbally. Participants can be more honest and open. Allowing a time of silence, with no expectation that anyone must say anything aloud, can be an effective prayer tool. With this approach people are able to say their own prayers in a way that is appropriate for them.

## 13. Altar Prayer

One effective way to use silent prayer is by allowing youth to go to the altar to pray. Many adolescents like altar prayer time. It gives them a chance to spend time in silent prayer in a structured way. The physical movement to and from the altar is also important. Soft background music and subdued lighting are ways of enhancing the mood or atmosphere. It is important not to rush altar prayer time. Most teens will pray for a minute or two, but occasionally someone will need a longer time. You may need to establish beforehand the expectation for the others to wait patiently and respectfully.

## 14. ACTS Prayers

ACTS is an acronym for four traditional ways of praying: adoration, confession, thanksgiving, and supplication. These four letters refer to the four types of content in the prayer—what it is we're talking about to God.

**A**—Adoration refers to praising God for who God is, as in "Dear God, you are a good God because. . . ." This form of prayer enables group members to practice praying by focusing on who God is and why God is special—rather than on themselves and their needs.

**C**—Confession refers to being open and honest before God about our own shortcomings, as in "Dear God, I am sorry that I. . . ." Confession is important because all of us carry hidden wounds, hurts, and guilt that need to be forgiven. It allows youth to seek forgiveness.

**T**—Thanksgiving refers to thanking God for what God has done in our lives, as in "Lord, I thank you for. . . ." This expression of gratitude is probably the most common form of prayer for youth and the easiest for them to do, but it still needs to be practiced. Prayers of thanksgiving allow us to be thankful and to be mindful of the fact that much of what we have comes from outside ourselves. It keeps us from being consumed by self.

**S**—Supplication refers to asking God for help, as in "Lord, help me to. . . ." The prayer can be for ourselves or for others. This prayer has a dual focus: the need and the source we turn to for help. Prayers of supplication teach humility and concern for others.

## 15. Eightfold Prayer

The eightfold prayer is similar to the ACTS prayer, except that the content of the prayer is divided into eight topics rather than four. Adoration, confession, and thanksgiving remain on the list. Supplication is divided into petition and intercession. And three more forms of prayer are added: aspiration, commitment, and acceptance.

**Adoration** (the same as in ACTS)

**Confession** (the same as in ACTS)

**Thanksgiving** (the same as in ACTS)

**Petition** refers to supplication for ourselves, as in "God, help me to. . .

**Intercession** refers to supplication for others, as in "God, help Tim to. . . ." Although similar, these two forms of supplication allow us to make a distinction between our needs and the needs of others. Both are appropriate but are distinctly different.

**Aspiration** refers to praying that we might become more like what God would have us to be, as in "Lord, help me to be more loving when. . . ." Aspiration is important because it allows us to focus on the ultimate goal of discipleship—to become more Christlike.

**Commitment** refers to dedicating ourselves to new attitudes and behaviors that go beyond what we have been in the past, as in "Lord, I commit myself to. . . ." Prayers of commitment allow us to focus on the heart of the Christian faith—our commitment to God and God's kingdom and our commitment to walk with God in our daily lives.

**Acceptance** refers to opening ourselves to receive what God would give us, as in "Jesus, I accept your forgiveness," or "Thy will be done." This is probably the hardest form of prayer. Although this form of prayer is difficult for most adults, it is not beyond the reach of youth.

## 16. Prayers and Concerns

This technique enables group members to voice their experiences—their ups and their downs, their joys and their concerns, their positive and negative experiences in a prayer time. These can he voiced in worship or in another setting. One variation is to have the group respond with a short phrase after each prayer so that the whole group participates in the prayer. Possible responses include "Lord, hear our prayer," or "This is our prayer, O Lord."

These responses are important for several reasons. At one level, they enable the group to participate in and affirm each prayer or concern. The response enables us to make one person's prayer our prayer.

At another level, the response clearly indicates when one prayer has ended and the group is ready to hear another. This is especially important in large groups, when an individual's prayer may not have been heard by everyone. In these settings, the leader can repeat the prayer or concern so that everyone can hear it and then lead the group in the response.

## 17. Prayer for Concerns

In this format, members of the group lift up their concerns by saying them aloud. As each concern is lifted up, another member of the group will agree to pray for that concern. This prayer can be voiced immediately after each concern, or it can be done in the closing prayer. If the closing prayer is a circle prayer, the people who agreed to pray for specific concerns do so as the prayer comes to them. In another form, the closing prayer begins in silence or with the statement "Let us pray . . . "; and then each person is free to add to the prayer, including those who have agreed to pray for specific concerns.

## 18. Journal Prayer

Journaling involves writing a diary to God. The person writes openly about his or her thoughts and feelings, as in a diary, except that God becomes the one to whom the diary is written. Or the diary could be turned into a spiritual growth journal. In this case, the content would be limited to things that affect the person's spiritual journey or relationship with God.

## 19. Letters to God

This is a variation of the prayer journal, in which members write a letter to God, much as they would write a letter to anyone else. They write about the things that they want to address—their concerns, hopes, struggles, and so on.

*"I never will forget the first time I journaled. It wasn't really hard. It was like writing in a diary, except I wrote to God. It helped me to see God like a person that I can talk and express myself to. I had never really thought about that before, Since the retreat where I learned this, I find that I occasionally still need to talk to God in this way. I don't do it all the time. But when I am really struggling with something, it helps."*

Carla, age 15

## 20. Dialogue Prayers

This technique is a modification of the letter to God (or Jesus). Group members begin a conversation by asking a question or making a statement and then continuing with what they think that God would say in response. The pattern continues as a dialogue or conversation.

Do not fear that someone might come up with some wildly distorted understandings of God. Having members read their dialogues within small groups. can care for that concern. The groups can correct any such wild statements. Usually a strong correlation emerges between what God says in these dialogue prayers and how God is presented in the Scriptures.

## 21. Prayer Partners

In this technique, two persons agree to pray together. Each will hear the concerns of the other, and then each will pray for those concerns. Each person may pray for his or her own concerns or for the other person's—either silently or aloud. They may pray holding hands.

The partners may also commit to continuing the prayers for each other during the time until they are together again. Some will choose a particular time when both will pray wherever they are.

## 22. Intensive-Care Units

The ICUs are small groups in which the members agree to be involved in a few minutes of intimate conversation and prayer. Some youth groups form ICUs during the opening or closing few minutes of their meeting time. In these small groups, the members speak openly and honestly about how they are doing and then pray for one another. In an ICU, it is important to take time to hear the concerns before praying. The prayers should be in response to the concerns and should mention them specifically.

## 23. Prayer and Share Groups

A prayer and share group is like an ICU, except that it lasts longer and is more in depth. A prayer and share group might meet for an hour or more. During that time, members talk about things that are important to them and the group tries to be loving and supportive. As a person finishes speaking, the group briefly prays for that person in light of what he or she expressed.

This type of group can take a variety of forms. Some groups let anyone join who wants to participate, since there is no set theme or agenda. Other groups are keyed to special needs and issues, such as divorce, death, life transitions (graduation, drivers license), parent/youth communication, and so forth.

## 24. Blessings and Bandages

In this exercise, one person chooses another member to hold his or her head. The person then lies on the floor, face up and eyes closed, with his or her head in the other member's lap. The others in the group place their hands on the person and then pray for that person. The person on the floor is not allowed to say anything until the exercise is over. This is an extremely powerful and is especially effective with people who feel that they are not important or that others do not care for them.

# CHAPTER

# PRAYER: LISTENING TO GOD

A s a freshman in high school, Erika went off for her first "quiet time" as part of a spirituality retreat. She was extremely skeptical about how she was going to use thirty minutes by herself. She also was keenly aware that following the solitude time, there would be ninety minutes of free time; and she was looking forward to being with her friends. Thirty minutes sounded like a long time to be by herself, but she was willing to give it a try.

Two hours later, an excited Erika couldn't wait to tell others the results of her time alone. She had spent the entire two hours by herself under a tree, reading a passage of Scripture, thinking about it, and writing a letter from God. She confessed that "it took the first thirty minutes just to get calm and put other things out of my mind. It was only then that I could really get into the exercise. Then the time flew." The letter from God, in which she expressed what she thought God might say to her, was based on the Scripture she had read. Through it, Erika was able to work on a key issue in her life that had been bothering her for some time—her estranged relationship with her father. For her, the letter was "an answered prayer." Years later, she still treasures the letter and its place in her life and in her spiritual life journey.

Tim was ecstatic: "That was cool! Can we do that again?" The "that" to which Tim referred was a guided imagery meditation in which he and several other junior high students had been invited to use their imagination to meet and have a conversation with Jesus on a seashore. The leader had walked the group slowly through the meditation, allowing plenty of time for them to use their imagination and fill in the blanks. Then the leader had invited the youth to visualize the scene as if they were there.

Both of these stories illustrate a whole dimension of spirituality often overlooked in our work with young people—listening to God.

## *The Loss of Listening to God*

All too often, the spiritual disciplines we have been taught focus on our talking to God rather than listening to God. We easily slip into a spirituality that focuses on what we do, rather than on what God does. We are called into a relationship with God. But a relationship requires two sides and two-way communication. A relationship based on one party doing all of the talking and not listening to the other is not much of a relationship.

The irony is that throughout the history of the Christian faith, there have been well-developed forms of prayer and Bible study that allow us to listen to what God is saying to us. But many in the church, including the youth, have had little contact with these prayer forms.

Historically, the church has affirmed two basic forms of prayer: active prayer, in which we talk to God, and passive (or dispositional) prayer in which we listen to God. Active prayer, which we examined in Chapter 2, includes most of the prayer forms we normally use: petition, intercession, thanksgiving, praise, confession, adoration. What all of these have in common is that they provide ways for us to express ourselves to God. Even when we are invited to a time of silent prayer, this is usually devoted to active prayer, spoken mentally rather than aloud.

Within our history, there is another prayer form, one that is devoted to learning how to dispose ourselves to listening to God. Recent physiological research and left brain/right brain theory reinforces this second approach. We now know that the two halves of the brain function in different ways. One side (the left) is analytical, logical, and rational. The other side is intuitive and imaginative. The spirituality with which most of us are familiar is left-brain spirituality—analytical and rational. We study the Bible. We address ourselves to God in active prayer. In a sense, we think aloud to God.

What is missing for many of us is right-brain spirituality—using our imagination and our intuition, as well as silence, to allow us to listen to what God may be saying to us. Historically, many of the ancient saints of the church used these right-brain prayer forms. Perhaps the best known was Ignatius of Loyola, the founder of the Jesuit order. Ignatius developed many of the tools described in the following pages.

This chapter is devoted to exploring how youth can be taught to listen to God. The injunction of the psalmist is "be still, and know that I am God" (Psalm 46:10). It has never been easy to put aside the cares and distractions that surround us; and in the modern world, it is becoming increasingly difficult. Yet young people have a natural affinity for these prayer forms and enjoy them immensely.

## *Dispositional Prayer: Key Definitions*

Dispositional prayer is the opposite of active prayer. Rather than providing a way for us to address or speak to God, dispositional prayer provides ways we can listen to God. It uses time-tested techniques that allow us to "dispose" ourselves to be open to God. We can't make God speak to us. But we can make ourselves ready to listen and attend to God's presence in our lives. There are two main forms of dispositional prayer: meditation and contemplation.

Although these two forms of dispositional prayer are often confused, they are actually the opposite of each other. Meditation is a technique in which we are invited to focus on something and then see what happens. We might meditate on a passage of Scripture. In that case, we would read the Scripture and then see what comes to mind. The idea is that God might speak through the free association that occurs in meditation. Meditation also can focus on a word, an image, or a variety of other objects.

Contemplation is the opposite of meditation. Instead of focusing on an object, the idea is to try to empty the mind of all content. Historically, this is called *kenosis,* or emptying. In contemplation, a person tries to let his or her mind go blank and then let God speak into the silence.

## *Components of Dispositional Prayer*

In working with youth, there are six basic components to using dispositional prayer. These six elements allow us to relax and dispose ourselves to be open to the actual prayer techniques.

### 1. Silence

To listen to God, a person must first be quiet. Speaking and all other activities need to cease. As long as we are talking, we are not listening. The first requirement for listening to God is a closed mouth. For many youth this will be a new experience. Fortunately, silence is a skill that can be learned. With time and experience, most youth can develop a real appreciation for a quiet time.

Mental quietness is also important and much more difficult to achieve. The techniques that follow are designed to occupy the mind so that it too can be silent. But ceasing to talk aloud is the beginning point.

*"Many times, my prayers can become so overcome with requests and hopes of God that I forget to listen for an answer. That's not to say that I hear God's voice in my head or anything. But if I am focused and my mind is free and clear, sometimes the answer will just come to me. I guess it's sort of like meditation, only I call it prayer. If I can just clear everything out of my head and just 'talk' to God, then the connection that is formed can often lead me to an answer. Many times when I choose not to listen to God, it's because I don't want to hear the answer. Many times, I try too hard to work through things on my own and 'take control' of my own life; but in the process, I lose the understanding that I need God in my life. And if I will only open my heart and my mind, I will hear God."*

Michelle, age 16

### 2. A Place Apart

The Gospels report that Jesus often went away from the crowds to "a place apart" to pray. Distractions are still a major barrier to listening to God. In order to listen to God, we need to find our own place apart, one that is free from distraction and interruptions.

In our world, this is increasingly difficult. In our day-to-day lives, we are rarely alone. For many of the youth we work with, this is further complicated by the presence of personal electronics that enable us to bring the world with us even when we are alone. To be "apart," we not only must be removed from the distractions of others around us, we also need to be free from the distractions we may bring with us.

When doing dispositional exercises, it is helpful to have young people remove themselves from any distractions. Sometimes this will require that each person goes off alone to an isolated place. In other situations, it may mean simply spreading out the youth throughout a room so that they are not touching one another and are as removed as possible from the distracting presence of others.

## 3. Breathing/Relaxing

Even when we have removed the distractions around us, we may still be preoccupied by the distractions within us. Like Erika, we may find that once we are alone, we are unable to relax. We may feel the tensions of the day or find our mind preoccupied with some of the thoughts we have tried to leave behind.

For thousands of years, people have used breathing exercises (breath work) and relaxation techniques to help center ourselves and release the cares we bring with us. This practice takes a variety of forms. One of the simplest techniques is to breathe slowly and deeply from the diaphragm. This exercise will increase the level of oxygen in the blood and make it less likely that a person will fall asleep during meditation. It also has a calming and relaxing effect on the body and the mind.

Another technique is to lie down and mentally go through the body, tightening and releasing various sets of muscles. You might start with the feet and then slowly move up to the head. As you come to each set of muscles, tighten and hold the muscles tight for about three seconds, and then release. Do this slowly and take about five to ten minutes to relax. Each person can do this on his or her own, or a leader can take the group through the relaxation exercise.

Other people like to "breathe Scripture." You can do this by taking a simple verse, such as "Be still, and know that I am God" (Psalm 46:10), and mentally repeating it over and over as you slowly breathe deeply in and out:

Be still (slow breath in),
and know (out)
that I (in)
am God (out).

Whatever technique is used, the point is that these breathing and relaxing exercises are not meditations in themselves. They are merely a way of relaxing and centering so that the person will be ready for the meditation.

## 4. Music

When we are quiet, we become aware of the distractions around us. There is traffic in the street. The stomach of the person next to us is making noises. In a group setting, we become aware of the noises others make around us. Soft, mellow music can be used to mask these distracting sounds. It functions much like "white noise." Any soft, relaxing music will do; but it is best if it does not have a definite rhythm and is not familiar. Rhythms and familiar pieces of music draw the listener's attention away from the meditation and into the music itself.

The best music is the kind that can be played in the background and not be noticed. A lot of music in the New Age section of the local music store can be used in this way. Some people object to anything with a "new age" label. But while new age philosophies and religious practices are often antithetical to Christian beliefs, much of the music in this section is not tied to the philosophy but is merely a contemporary form of soft music. Originally, this type of music was labeled "anti-frantic."

Some Christian artists, such as John Michael Talbot and Fernando Ortega, have composed music specifically for Christian meditation. Some contemporary praise and worship music also works well for meditation, as does soft jazz. Much of the music under the labels Narada, Private Music, and Windham Hill is very helpful. You can create a desired mood for a meditation by selecting music to go with the meditation. Some youth leaders have made soundtracks for meditations by linking several pieces of music together.

## 5. Using the Imagination

One of the key elements for dispositional prayer is the use of the imagination. In dispositional prayer, individuals are invited to use their imagination to enter into a passage of Scripture, a story, or an image. The imagination becomes the vehicle by which the person can cut off the outside world and explore the inner world.

During the meditation techniques below, it is important that everyone be allowed to use his or her imagination. The instructions should be minimal and suggestive. When leading a meditation for others, we need to set it up so that persons use their imagination. And we should avoid anything that hampers the imagination.

## 6. Adequate Time

Dispositional prayer takes time. For Erika, it took thirty minutes just to get to the point where she could do the exercise. If she had given up after twenty minutes or so, she never would have had the experience she did. Dispositional prayer cannot be rushed or controlled. The idea is to dispose ourselves by using the elements discussed in this section so that the techniques mentioned below can have a chance to work. Adequate time, without rushing, is crucial.

## *Techniques for Dispositional Prayer*

### Guided Experience of Scriptures

One of the most powerful tools for dispositional prayer is guided meditation on Scripture. Although specifically designed to help make the Scriptures come to life, the elements developed by Ignatius centuries ago lend themselves readily to other techniques. In its Bible study form, the technique is a way of enabling the individual to move beyond simply reading the biblical story. It enables the person to enter into the story as a full participant so that what happened in the story happens to the person doing the meditation. In an Ignatian meditation there are four keys:

1. Use your five senses to experience what is happening in the story. What do you see? hear? taste? touch? smell? Focus on the story and the scene. Use each sense to make the story come alive. What colors do you see? Can you feel the wind? the sun? What conversation could you have heard? The list is endless.

**61**

2. Use your imagination to enter into the story and become a part of the scene. Imagine yourself in the story. You are there. Go through the story as a participant. Become a part of the story. Don't read the narrative as a detached, objective outsider. Read it as one who is intimately involved with what is going on.

3. Identify with the story emotionally. What would you have felt if you had been there? How would what is happening affect you? What are your reactions? What specific emotions does the story evoke?

4. Become one of the characters in the story. Choose a character, or just let yourself gravitate naturally to one of the characters. Experience the story from the perspective of the person in the story. Or better yet, experience the story from more than one character's perspective. Experiencing the story from the perspective of each character gives a richness to the story that we otherwise miss.

There are two ways to approach an Ignatian meditation. The first is to go through a passage of Scripture several times. The person reads the passage one time for each of the five senses. Each time, the person focuses on a different sense to experience the story from that perspective. Then the story is read a sixth time and the reader places herself or himself within the story. Then the story is read one final time, and the reader becomes one or more characters in the story.

The second approach may be more helpful in youth ministry. In this approach, a leader takes a group through the meditation. The participants lie on the floor as the leader takes them through the breathing exercises and the meditation. In this form, the various dimensions of the meditation are done simultaneously by the leader. The people are invited to enter into the story, and the leader provides the hints that help them become involved. The following meditations can give an idea of how this is done:

**Example: John 1:35-39 (Jesus calls his first disciples.)**
Relax. . . . Take a series of slow deep breaths. . . . In. . . . Out. . . . In. . . . Out. . . . Imagine that you are living 2,000 years ago in the land of Israel. . . . You live near Jerusalem. . . . You have heard of this new prophet, called Jesus. . . . But you have never met him. . . . It's late in the afternoon. . . . You're standing with two other people. . . . Look around for a moment at the scene. . . . What can you see? . . . Feel the wind, . . . the warmth of the sun. . . . Listen to the sounds around you. . . . Smell the air. . . . What are you feeling as you stand there? . . . You see a man in the distance, walking toward you. . . . The man looks unfamiliar. . . . But there seems to be something special about him. . . . What do you sense about this man? . . . One of the two people you have been standing with is John the Baptist. . . . What does he look like? . . . What is it like being there with him? . . . Why are you there? . . . John now points to the man walking toward you and says, "Look, there is the Lamb of God." . . . What does John mean by this? . . . What do you feel? . . . As Jesus walks by, you and John and the other person who was with you begin to follow Jesus. . . . Why are you following Jesus? . . . Jesus now turns around and looks at you. . . . What does he look like? . . . What expression do you see on his face? . . . What are you feeling as Jesus looks at you? . . . What are you thinking? . . . Jesus then asks you, "What do you want?" . . . Answer him. . . . You ask him where he lives. . . . Jesus then says, "Come and see." . . . Why do you want to know where Jesus is living? . . . Why does Jesus want you to go

with him? . . . What is it you will see if you follow? . . . You begin to follow Jesus to where he is going. . . . What do you see as you journey with him? . . . Who else is around? . . . And how are they reacting to him? . . . How are you reacting? . . . You come to the house where Jesus is staying. . . . Take a few moments to look at the house and the people with whom Jesus is staying. . . . You spend the rest of the day at the home with Jesus. . . . What do you do? . . . What do you talk about? . . .

(Allow a few minutes for a conversation to take place.) . . . Bring your awareness back into this room, to this time and place. . . . What stands out from the meditation you just went through? . . . What is it that you want from Jesus? . . . What is it that you find when Jesus invites you to "come and see"? . . . What did you talk about with Jesus?

### Example: John 3:1-8 (Nicodemus comes to Jesus at night.)

You are in the city of Jerusalem at the time Jesus was alive. . . . You're walking down a street late at night. . . . You are alone. . . . You have heard about this new prophet, Jesus from Galilee. . . . He is in your town. . . . What thoughts and feelings does his being here stir up? . . . You are a religious leader. . . . You have been raised in your faith. . . . You know the Bible, and others respect you. . . . You are going to meet Jesus. . . . You are going at night because you don't want your friends to know that you are going to see him. . . . Why are you going to meet Jesus? . . . What is it you want? . . . Why are you going alone, at night? . . . Of what are you afraid? . . . You're walking down a dark street. . . . What do you see? . . . What do you hear? . . . What is the temperature like? . . . Can you smell anything? . . . What emotions are going through you? . . . Ahead, in a courtyard, are a group of people. They are gathered around a fire, talking. . . . One of them has his back to you. . . . Somehow, you sense that this is the person for whom you are looking. . . . What goes through your mind as you get close to him? . . . He turns to look at you and smiles. . . . What does he look like? . . . He doesn't say anything. . . . How do you feel? . . . What will you say? . . . You find yourself giving Jesus a compliment. . . . You tell him how much you have heard about him, . . . how he must be a great teacher to be able to do the things he does, . . . how he must be from God. . . . Now Jesus speaks. . . . He speaks directly to you. . . . But his comment doesn't seem to fit anything. . . . He doesn't seem to acknowledge your compliment. . . . Instead, he says something strange. . . . He says, "Unless you are born again, you cannot see the kingdom of God." . . . Take a few moments for these words to sink in. . . . What does he mean? . . . And why is he saying this to you? . . . You find yourself confused. . . . You fumble for words and mumble something about how it is impossible for someone your age to be physically born a second time. . . . Jesus now speaks a second time. . . . He seems to sense your confusion. . . . He adds, "Unless you are born through water and the Spirit, you cannot enter the kingdom of God. Don't be surprised when I say that you must be born from above. Remember, the Spirit of God blows wherever it pleases; you hear it, but you can't tell where it is coming from or where it is going. That is how it is with all who are born of the Spirit." . . . For a few moments, engage Jesus in a conversation about what he means. . . . Find out why he is saying these things to you. . . . Why does he keep saying, "You cannot enter the kingdom of God unless . . . "?

## Guided Imagery Meditation

In a guided imagery meditation, Ignatian techniques are used, but the meditation is no longer just an exploration of a biblical story or scene. Guided imagery meditations take the Scripture text as a point of departure and then expand on an element in the story. The following meditation is based on Jesus' parable found in Matthew 13:45-46: "Again, the kingdom of heaven is like a merchant looking for fine pearls; on finding one pearl of great value, he went and sold all that he had and bought it."

The idea of a valuable pearl representing God's gift of the kingdom becomes the point of departure. In the meditation, the listeners are invited to imagine encountering Jesus on a seashore and having Jesus give them a "pearl of great price." The listeners provide the content to the pearl. The leader merely sets the story up so that the listeners have a chance to use their imagination to explore what it is that God is giving.

### Example: Matthew 13:45-46 (The Pearl of Great Price)

Imagine that you are walking along a seashore. . . . It's late at night, but the moon shines brightly. . . . Take a few moments just to enjoy the scene. . . . Look out over the ocean. . . . Listen to the sound of the crashing waves. . . . Feel the waves as the surf comes over your feet. . . . Feel the cool evening breeze. . . . You are walking down by the seashore because something is troubling you. . . . Something is not right in your life or is missing. . . . What is it that brings you to the seashore, alone, late at night? . . . You see in the distance a figure walking toward you. . . . As the figure comes closer, you sense that this is no ordinary person. . . . There is something special about this person. . . . Something tells you that somehow, for some reason, Jesus is walking toward you. . . . What does he look like? . . . Why is he here? . . . Why is he walking toward you? . . . What do you feel? . . . As he approaches, you stop at the edge of the surf. . . . Without saying anything, Jesus walks over beside you and looks into your eyes. . . . He seems to know you. . . . He senses what is going on inside you. . . . He knows your struggle, your pain, what is missing in your life. . . . Jesus smiles. . . . He reaches down into the surf and pulls out a strange looking shell. . . . It looks like a clam. . . . Jesus opens the shell and holds it up for you to look at. . . . Inside the clam is something that looks like a large pearl. . . . But it is unlike any pearl you have ever seen. . . . Look closely at it. . . . Look into it. . . . It is clear. . . . Looking into it is almost like looking into a window. . . . You sense that if you look into it carefully, you will be able to see something. . . . You look up at Jesus, . . . into his eyes. . . . You sense care and warmth. . . . You sense that Jesus has a gift for you. . . . If you look deeply into the strange pearl, you will see the gift that God has to give you. . . . You look at the pearl. . . . Jesus places the strange pearl in your hand. . . . You gaze deeply into it. . . . You see. . . . Take a few moments to really look at what is in the pearl. . . . What is it that you see? . . . Why is this important to you? . . . What is God's gift to you. . . . What is Jesus offering you? . . . Look back at Jesus. . . . Take a few moments to tell him what his gift means to you. . . . Look again into the pearl. . . . You look up, and Jesus is gone. . . . You are standing alone on the beach, but the pearl is still in your hand. . . . God's gift to you is still there. . . .

End with a brief prayer in which you thank God for the gift you have received.

## Guided Fantasy

A guided fantasy uses Ignatian techniques but is totally devoid of any contact with Scripture. Here the leader sets up a fantasy in which the person gets to meet God or Jesus or have some lived experience that invites the person into reflecting on his or her relationship with God. This idea is as old as Plato's famous cave scene in *The Republic,* where God is encountered.

The following fantasy was suggested by the science-fiction movie *Brainstorm,* in which a person has an afterlife experience and is brought back. This fantasy takes the medical technology suggested in the movie and uses it as a vehicle for an afterlife experience in which the person has a direct experience of God.

### Example: A Life-After-Death Experience

It's late at night, and you are being taken to a secret military installation. . . . A short time ago, a group of people came to your house and said that they needed your help with a secret experiment. . . . And now you are at the installation. . . . You walk inside. . . . What are you feeling? . . . What do you see? . . . You enter a strange room. . . . The walls are lined with strange electronic equipment. . . . In the middle of the room is a platform for someone to lie on. . . . A man in a white coat thanks you for coming. . . . He repeats what he said earlier. . . . They are doing experiments on life-after-death experiences. . . . The equipment can suspend all life functions—heart beating, breathing—so that a person can technically "die" then be brought back to life. . . . They want your help because you are a Christian. . . . They said that the last person who went through this experiment claimed to have met God. . . . They want you to go through the experiment and then tell what you experience after you die. . . . You hear yourself agree. . . . You are on the platform. . . . They are giving you a shot. . . . You find yourself drifting off. . . . Then nothing. . . . You have the sensation of floating. . . . You can't see anything . . . or feel anything. . . . You see in the distance a dim light. . . . You find yourself moving toward the light. . . . You begin to feel excited as you draw closer. . . . There is something special about this light. . . . As you come closer, other lights begin to appear and fly around you. . . . You hear something that sounds like music. . . . In the center of all the lights and music is the light you first saw. . . . You are getting very close. . . . You feel a warm, tingling sensation all over. . . . You sense that you are floating in the presence of God. . . . Inside your head, there is a voice. . . . It is the voice of God. . . . God speaks to you and says. . . . You feel. . . . Feel God's love like the warmth of the sun. . . . Feel God's care like a wind that blows across your body. . . . Tell God how you are feeling. . . . You feel yourself now being drawn back. . . . Somehow you know that the experiment is over, and you have to return. . . . What will you take with you from these few moments. . . . What will you say when you are back in the room?

### Example: Meeting God in a Cave (This fantasy develops Plato's idea of meeting God in a cave.)

You're walking through a forest. . . . You can see the sun up above breaking through the leaves. . . . Beams of light strike the ground around you. . . . You feel the coolness of a breeze. . . . You hear the sound of a small stream nearby. . . . A small animal runs past you. . . . A bird flies overhead and cries out. . . . Up ahead, you can see a cave. . . .

You walk over to it. . . . You look inside. . . . You feel a cool breeze coming out of the cave. . . . You put your hand on the side of the cave to guide you as you walk in. . . . You walk farther and farther. . . . It is very dark and quiet. . . . As your eyes slowly adjust, you see some kind of light in the distance. . . . You slowly begin to walk toward the light. . . . The cave turns to the right. . . . The light seems to be coming from around the turn. . . . You go around the corner and see. . . . You are in a large chamber of the cave. . . . In the center of the chamber is something unlike anything you have ever seen before. . . . It is a light, a flame, or something. . . . It is hovering in the air. . . . It is moving around. . . . You suddenly become aware that the room is pleasantly warm. . . . You feel a tingling on your skin. . . . A chill goes up your spine. . . . There is something about this light. . . . It's almost alive. . . . Then somehow you sense that you are in the presence of God. . . . Somehow God is present with you . . . in this room . . . in this flame. . . . You feel. . . . What thoughts are going through your mind? . . . Suddenly, a voice seems to be inside your head. . . . It speaks to you and says. . . . You say. . . . The voice invites you to ask any questions you have. . . . You think for a moment then ask. . . . Suddenly, the light begins to grow, . . . to fill the room. . . . You can feel the gentle warmth of the light all over your body. . . . The light seems to go right through you. . . . You feel loved, . . . complete. . . . And now it is time to go. . . . You start to leave. . . . You turn back one last time and say. . . . Then you slowly leave the cave. . . . You are aware that you have changed. . . . The experience in the cave has had an effect on you. . . . It is. . . . You are different because. . . .

## Conversation With God/Jesus

This idea was suggested and developed in the book *No Instant Grapes in God's Vineyard,* by Louise Spiker. The basic idea is the same as the Ignatian exercises, mentioned earlier, except that the person writes down his or her thoughts, feelings, and experiences on a sheet of paper. Begin with a question or statement to God (or Jesus) and then write down what you think God (Jesus) might say in response. Then respond to God's (or Jesus') comment. Continue in the form of a conversation between you and what you honestly think God would say to your questions and statements.

One approach is to read a passage of Scripture first, then let the Scripture set the tone and boundaries of the conversation. In this instance, you would write down what you think God would say in light of how God is depicted in that Scripture.

Another approach is not to limit God's comment to a passage of Scripture but to honestly write down what you think God might say, based on everything you know about God.

### Example: A Conversation With Jesus

**Me:** Jesus, I've been struggling with what I am going to do with my life.

**Jesus:** Tell me about the struggle.

**Me:** There are so many things I could do. But I'm not sure which I really want to do or which is best.

**Jesus:** God has given you talents and abilities. What do these tell you?

**Me:** Well, I'm good with people. I enjoy them. I seem to get along well with people, and they seem to like me.

**Jesus:** How could you use this ability?

**Me:** In lots of different ways. But I would also like to make a good living. I would like to be able to afford all the good things of life.

**Jesus:** Have I taught you anything that would help you with this?

**Me:** Well, I know that money isn't everything.

**Jesus:** Can it make you happy?

**Me:** It's important, but I know that it isn't everything.

**Jesus:** How does that help you make a decision about your future?

**Me:** I know that I shouldn't decide just based on how much I will earn.

**Jesus:** On what will you base your decision?

**Me:** On what I know I can do well. And on what makes me happy.

**Jesus:** What about others? Should you think about other people and the world around you when you make this kind of decision?

**Me:** I'm not sure.

**Jesus:** Will your decision affect others?

**Me:** I guess so. I know that I could do something that would help others and make the world a better place.

**Jesus:** That's a thought.

**Me:** It is. It's an important thought.

*"Listening to God for me has always been one of my biggest challenges. I tend to try so hard to do everything on my own, that it takes some big event for me to turn to God for help. But more recently, I have started to understand that there are a lot more times in my life when God is trying to talk to me; and I'm just not there to listen. We go through life with varying awareness levels of God; and often it is only when we need God the most, that God seems to come through for us. But that's not true; God's presence is there all the time. It is more a matter of us opening ourselves up to hear God's call. Listening to God does not take self-effort. Instead, it takes a willingness to let go of your own feeble attempts to seek out God's answers. For it is only when we truly stop trying to do it all ourselves, and allow ourselves to fall into God's tranquility and peace, that we are really able to grasp what God wants for us in life."*

Danny, age 17

## Letters to God and Letters From God

Here is another idea developed by Louise Spiker. In the case of letters to God or letters from God, the same idea is followed, except that the thoughts are developed in letter form, rather than in a dialogue. A person writes a long letter to God (much like a "Dear Abby" letter) in which the person explores his or her thoughts and feelings in some depth. Then the person writes a letter in which God responds ("Dear Abby" style) to the first letter. The key here is to be as faithful as possible to what you honestly think God would say. In the above example, a person would explore the same issue but in letter form.

## Meditating on Scripture

In meditating on Scripture, a person reads a passage slowly and carefully, making notes on anything that gets his or her attention. Then, with those notes as background, the person meditates—reflects, thinks, ponders, free-associates—on what the Scripture said. The person may meditate mentally and write down only what stands out. Or the person may write the entire meditation on paper, carefully recording the thoughts and feelings that he or she becomes aware of. The meditation then takes on a life of its own, and the thoughts hook other thoughts. In a true meditation, the person does not know where the meditation will lead. The idea is that the Scripture becomes the starting point for a journey.

## Meditation on a Word or an Image

The same process described above can be used in a variety of ways. The person may want to meditate on a key word, such as *love,* or *grace,* or *Jesus,* or *God*—or on an image, such as the cross in the sanctuary, a picture of Jesus' crucifixion, or a sunset. In this type of meditation, the image or word becomes the starting point. It leads the meditators beyond themselves to a reflection on some aspect of their relationship with God.

## Creative Imaging

In creative imaging, a person uses an image to make God's presence more real. God is present with us all the time. God's presence is like the air we breathe and the sun—always there but rarely in our awareness. With a little creativity, God's presence can be compared to something a person experiences all the time.

### Example: Sun on the Body

This imaging works best if the group members are outside and can feel the sun's rays on their skin or clothing. Have them close their eyes and feel the warmth of the sun's rays for a few moments. Then have them imagine that the rays of the sun are an expression of God's love for them. The warmth they feel is the warmth of God's love. Have them experience this for a few moments; then ask them to give a mental prayer to God, giving thanks for God's love.

### Example: Wind on the Body

This imaging technique is similar to the one above, in that it works best outdoors. Have the students feel the wind in their hair, on their face, and on their skin. The amount of wind is not really important. A strong breeze can express God's power. A gentle breeze can express the caressing of God's presence. Have the group members experience the wind for a few moments, then have them think about the wind as an expression of God's Spirit. You might want to mention that the Old Testament word for Spirit, *ruah,* also means *wind* and *breath.* Have them experience the wind as *ruah,* as God's Spirit, or breath.

### Example: Breathing

The group can also link God's Spirit to breathing. Have the teens close their eyes and become aware of their breathing. Have them feel the air going in and out of their bodies, giving life and oxygen. Link the breathing they are doing to the Hebrew word *ruah,* for breath. Remind them that God "breathed" life into Adam in the Creation story. Then have them imagine the breath they feel as the Spirit of God flowing into them, giving them life.

**Example: Blood in Veins**

Have the group members feel the blood flowing through their veins. They can do this either by feeling their pulse or by becoming very still and feeling their hearts beat. They should be able to feel the flowing of blood through various parts of their bodies. Have them mentally imagine the blood flowing around and around in their bodies, giving them life. Then have them imagine God's love for them as that blood. Have them experience this image for a couple of minutes.

## Contemplation

Contemplation, or "emptying" prayer, is more difficult than meditation. It is a learned skill that requires practice. Junior high students often find this difficult, but many senior highs may find it helpful. In contemplation, one finds a place to be alone and tries to the best of his or her ability to go mentally blank. It is normal for this to be difficult. All kinds of random thoughts will come to mind—tasks we need to do, places we need to go.

Contemplation is best when it is coupled with breath work and journaling. Ask those who want to experience contemplation to take a few minutes for relaxation and breathing exercises. Then have them close their eyes and try to go blank. Explain that they are to expect difficulty with this exercise. Have them spend about thirty minutes trying to be empty. At the end of this exercise, ask them to journal what they experienced. They may have had physical sensations, seen lights or patterns behind their eyelids, had interesting thoughts pass through their minds.

Some contemplators like to read a passage of Scripture or look at a symbol, such as a cross, just before they contemplate. For some, this is helpful as a point of focus. Contemplation is not for everyone; but some people, including teenagers, find it helpful. It can produce insights. At a minimum, it can be a very relaxing time.

## Mystic Prayer

Mystic prayer is a form of meditation in which one deliberately tries to feel at one with God or God's creation. Many people have occasional paranormal experiences in which they feel at one with the universe or with God. Some people find looking at a sunset or some other work of nature to be helpful. Others turn contemplation into mystic prayer. The joys of mystic prayer are those rare moments when we feel a profound sense of "at-one-ment" with God or God's creation.

## *The Power of Dispositional Prayer*

Dispositional prayer adds a whole new dimension to our spiritual life and the spiritual life of the young people with whom we work. In spiritual growth it is important to move beyond learning about God and to move toward ways we can have direct experiences of God. Like music and many forms of worship, dispositional prayer is more experiential than cognitive. It is learning to be in God's presence.

Some youth have a certain amount of initial resistance to dispositional prayer. The main reason seems to be that it is new and unfamiliar. Yet when they are exposed to many of the prayer forms in this chapter, they enjoy the activities and find them helpful in developing a sense of God's presence in their lives.

# WORSHIP

S everal older members of the congregation swore that there never had been (and never would be) any "dancing" in Sunday morning worship. They didn't like the idea of young women parading around "half naked" in front of the congregation. It was too sexual.

When the youth worship committee heard this concern being voiced in some of the adult Sunday school classes, they decided to go ahead and keep the planned dance in their Sunday youth service. But they made some significant changes. In the bulletin, the activity was called "liturgical movement." The five "dancers" were all modestly dressed and were all junior high students.

The group was in front of the congregation three times during the worship service—once when they "signed" the Scripture, once to do "liturgical movement" to a song, and once to provide interpretative movements to the creed. After the service, members of the congregation—including some of those who had been skeptical—gave high praise to the beauty and power of the worship service. Since that first service, the youth group has continued to include liturgical dance in its worship leadership, including several times when it was invited to provide movement for special services.

## The Cross

The highlight of junior high camp that year was the worship committee's decision to portray the Crucifixion by putting Marta on the cross. The focal point of the camp was Vesper Point, an outdoor worship area with a large wooden cross more than twenty feet tall. The committee

71

had decided that on the last night of camp, they wanted to focus in a powerful way on the meaning of the crucifixion of Jesus.

At the beginning of the service, two adults put a tall ladder up to the cross, and Marta slowly climbed the ladder until she was in position. She never said a word, but the entire service took place as the sun set behind Marta on the cross. Something about her silent presence there gave a whole new meaning to the crucifixion drama that night. As the songs were sung, the Scriptures read, and the drama acted out, Marta's silent witness bore testimony to the significance of the service. Years later, people who were there that evening would still point to that service as one of the most memorable they had ever attended.

## The Wall

The summer after the Berlin Wall came down, a group of senior high students were discussing what to do in the closing worship for their retreat. They had been discussing the various walls that separate them from God and from one another. They decided to make their theme "The Wall."

Before the service, they constructed a large wall of butcher paper. The wall, when erected, was about ten feet high and more than twenty feet long. They had drawn bricks on it to make it look more real. At the beginning of the service the wall was put up in front of the worship area. It completely blocked the view of the cross.

At one point in the service, the two hundred young people present were invited to take markers and write on the wall some things that separated them from God, from their families, and from others. Other participants spoke of the walls in their own lives. Later in the service, one person read aloud Ephesians 1:14, in which Paul speaks of Christ tearing down the wall that separates us from God and one another.

The participants were then invited to go up and take pieces of the wall, which represented barriers in their own lives, as a way of affirming God's power to overcome these obstacles. The image that many remembered years later was of the wall slowly crumbling and the cross emerging behind it. At the end, the wall was gone, the cross was visible, and each person had a piece of the wall to take home.

## The Testimonies

The senior pastor confessed that he had never heard anything like it in his twenty years of ministry. As part of a Sunday morning worship service, four young people of the church had stood up and given testimonies about their faith. The testimonies were not dramatic or shocking. They revealed no great sins. But they were from the heart.

One after another, they had stood up before the congregation and shared their faith. They talked about what it was like to grow up in the congregation, what it was like to be new to the church and to be warmly received, how it felt to experience God's presence for the first time at a camp, and what it was like to represent God and the church on a mission trip.

The pastor was supposed to follow this presentation with a brief sermon. After the last youth sat down, the pastor confessed that anything he could say would only detract from what had already been said.

## *The Missing* E

The youth group was having a serious problem, and the youth fellowship worship committee had decided to deal with the issue in that evening's worship service. Some members of the group had dropped out and become inactive. Others felt unappreciated or unimportant. The committee wanted to use Paul's analogy of the body in 1 Corinthians 12, but the real breakthrough came when someone read aloud a poem called "The Missing *E*." The poem had one letter missing—there were no *E*s. Each place where there was supposed to be an *E* was just a blank space. The result was that the poem made no sense. Removing one letter made that much difference. This became the organizing idea for the service.

At the service, the group dealt head-on with the problem it was having. Several members revealed what they were seeing and why it concerned them. Someone read aloud 1 Corinthians 12. Copies of "The Missing *E*" poem were handed out, and the group read it in silence. One member of the worship committee then invited everyone for a time of prayer at the attar rail.

On the altar were a paper sack and a basket. The worship leader stated that the solution to the problem was in the sack. As the members finished a time of prayer and personal reflection, they were invited to look into the sack at God's solution to the problem and then take one of the items from the basket. When the group members came to the altar and looked into the bag, they had a variety of reactions. Some smiled, some laughed, others stared for several moments. A few cried. Each person then took one of the small objects in the basket and sat down.

In the sack, the committee had placed an eight-inch, circular mirror, as a reminder that each person there was both the source of the problem and the key to the solution. From the basket, each person picked up a small mirror with an *E* written on it. After that night's service, the "problem" the group had been experiencing went away. Years later, members of the group confessed that they still had their small mirrors with the *E*.

## *The Bracelet*

Everyone remembered the time when the youth group almost disbanded. Divisions and cliques had formed. Some members stopped coming, and others openly announced that they didn't miss them. Attendance dropped from eighty members to fewer than twenty. Several of the adult sponsors admitted that they were discouraged and planned to stop working with the group. Even the youth minister confessed that for the first time in his ministry, he was considering whether his leaving might help the group.

When the youth council discussed the problem, they quickly decided that the most effective way to deal with the problem was in a worship service during the Sunday evening youth fellowship. The group valued worship. It was a setting where they would be the most likely to listen. The group planned the service and then sent a letter to all the young people in the church, inviting them to the worship event and explaining briefly what was at stake. The letter also went to all those who had stopped attending the youth group and church.

That night, more than 100 young people and sponsors showed up. People who had not been seen in months were present. In the middle of the service, several people on the youth council expressed their concerns, their feelings, and their fears. Then they opened up the discussion to the group. In the setting of worship, the group members began to express their pain and frustration. Then the mood turned to confession. No one wanted to lose what he or she had in the youth group, yet everyone felt that the end was near.

Then a member of the worship committee read a passage of Scripture on covenant and invited the members of the group to make a covenant with God and with one another to make the group what it could be—to make a new beginning. The group was invited to a time of prayer at the altar. Each member who was willing to make a new beginning was invited to put on a black-and-white bracelet that one of the adults had braided for the occasion. Black symbolized the death of what was. White symbolized rebirth. Three people left the room. Others went to the altar to pray.

After several minutes, one person put on a bracelet. Then another. And another. During the next fifteen minutes, all of the people who had stayed had put on bracelets. It was a turning point. The youth council was right. Worship was the right place to face the problem and recommit to solving it.

The characteristic that all of the services above have in common is that they were fully planned and led by youth. Adults helped by facilitating, but the young people provided the main ideas and the leadership.

Those of us who work with youth know they can plan powerful services. Many of the most moving worship experiences I have ever had have taken place in services planned and led by youth. This chapter will explore how worship can be a vital part of our ministry with youth and a central part of teenagers' spiritual growth.

## *What Worship Is*

Worship is at the very center of what it means to be a Christian. Whenever the church has gathered, it has gathered to worship. There is no church and no Christian community without worship. In the same way, our spiritual growth is anchored in worship. Worship renews our spirit. It strengthens and feeds us spiritually. In worship, we are comforted, challenged, forgiven, fed, and educated.

Worship has formational power. It shapes and molds. We are called to be transformed into the image of Christ. Worship is one of the "means of grace" God has given us that can enable that transformation. In worship, God—though the Holy Spirit—is at work in the body of Christ.

In our work with youth, especially in our attempts to help teens grow in their relationship with God, worship is central. It is not just another tool for our work with youth. In many ways, worship is the very soul of all we are about.

Definitions for *worship* vary. One seminary textbook on worship traces the word back to the old Anglo-Saxon word for *worth*. Much of our contemporary praise worship derives from this understanding. The real heart of worship is a desire to praise God, to ascribe worth to God, to acknowledge who God is. In this sense, worship is an activity through which we give honor to God, who is worthy of our adoration. The current edition of *The American Heritage Dictionary* gives three definitions that describe the essence of Christian worship:

- Reverent love and devotion accorded to a deity, an idol, or sacred object
- The ceremonies, prayers, or other religious forms by which this love is expressed
- Ardent devotion; adoration

Christian worship has several components. Each conveys an important dimension of worship:

## Christian Worship Is Corporate

Worship is different from private devotion. An individual can pray, read Scripture, sing songs, or do many of the activities that are done in worship. But it is not worship unless the community is gathered. Worship is, by definition, corporate. Worship is an act of the community, not the act of an individual. Worship doesn't need to involve the whole community. A church can have several services, including one at the evening youth fellowship meeting. But to be worship, the community needs to be present in some form.

## Christian Worship Is God-Directed

Even though worship is a human activity, it is directed to God. God is the object of worship. Worship differs from many human activities in that it does not focus on us. Rather, worship's focus is on God—on who God is, on how God is with us, on what God calls us to be. This radical God-directedness can be seen clearly in a lot of our contemporary praise worship.

## Christian Worship Is Christ-Centered

Christian worship, as distinct from other forms of worship, is centered in the revelation of God in Christ. It is not just God who is the focus. It is God as revealed in Jesus Christ. Our worship has a particular understanding of who God is. It focuses on how God is made known in the life and ministry of Jesus.

## Christian Worship Is Biblically-Based

The Scriptures are the ultimate source of our understanding of God and Jesus. Worship is anchored in the biblical revelation of God. In ancient times worship was based on sacrifice. But when the Jewish people returned from the Exile in the fifth century B.C.E., they brought with them a new form of worship, a form based not on the sacrifice of animals but on the reading and interpretation of Scripture. The eighth chapter of the Book of Nehemiah beautifully captures this moment. From that moment on we were a people of the Book. As Christians we continue that tradition. We, too, are a people of the Book.

The heart of any worship service is the reading of Scripture and the contemporary proclamation of its message in some way. Worship cannot be cut off from the Scriptures. If it is, it is cut adrift from its anchor.

## Christian Worship Is Context-Sensitive

Worship is not only anchored in the historical revelation of God in the Bible. It is also context-sensitive. Worship is always done by a particular group of people in a particular time and place. Karl Barth, the famous theologian, once made the comment that a Christian preacher should always approach the pulpit with a Bible under one arm and the daily newspaper under the other. A worshiping congregation exists at a specific place, in a specific time. It has specific needs and concerns, and worship addresses them specifically.

Youth worship speaks to the needs of youth. It addresses their concerns and issues. It is appropriate to youth. As such, it will be different in some respects from worship geared to adults. In the same way, if a worship service is geared to the whole congregation on Sunday morning, it must include the concerns and issues of youth to be authentic worship.

## Christian Worship Is Participatory

Worship is not a spectator sport. It is liturgy—"the work of the people." Worship is, by its very nature, participatory. Youth worship should involve youth in planning, in leading; and those who are not leading should be actively involved in whatever is going on. Just as adults cannot "do" worship for youth, youth worship leaders (even those who lead) cannot "do" worship for the congregation. Everyone present must be actively involved.

## Christian Worship Is Spirit-Led

There is a mystery about worship. It is a human activity. We plan it. We lead it. Yet the best worship experiences happen when the worship becomes more than we had planned. There are those moments when the Spirit of God seems to take over and move within a group. The sense of being led may happen in the planning or in the worship service itself. It is helpful to remember that the worship service is God's, not ours. And it is at its best when we get out of the Spirit's way and let the Spirit move within the service.

## *Involving Youth in Sunday Morning Services*

Participation in the main Sunday morning worship service is and will continue to be the main issue for worship with youth. Sunday morning is when the community gathers. For most churches, it may be the only time during the week when the church comes together as a total congregation. If the young people of the congregation are not vitally involved in Sunday morning services, they are cut off from the congregation's worship as a total body. We may provide other opportunities for youth to worship, but there is no substitute for participation as part of the body of Christ in the Sunday morning services.

Young people are a part of the congregation. They are not just "the future of the church." Although well intentioned, the real implication of this oft-quoted comment is that they are "not the present of the church." Nothing could be further from the truth. Not only do young people benefit from a worship that is sensitive to their needs, but they also have a lot to contribute to worship.

In many local churches, the teenagers are marginalized in Sunday morning worship. They are not included in any meaningful way. The sermons do not speak to them and their concerns. The music is alien to them; the liturgy, unengaging. They are asked to be passive participants. Yet in many other congregations, youth are involved in dynamic ways. We need to find ways for the services we offer to speak to youth as well as ways for youth to become involved in the services as leaders.

## Involving Youth as Participants

The pastor's relationship with the youth of the congregation is a crucial factor. Young people are relational. If they feel they know the person who is speaking, they will be more attentive and involved. If they feel that the pastor is a stranger, they will have little reason for focusing on what he or she says. What happens outside the pulpit affects the way what is said from the pulpit is received.

The pastor or worship leader can do much that will help teens feel that they belong. Most of these things are very simple; yet collectively, they can make a difference:

1. **Refer to youth and youth concerns in the sermons**. If the speaker is knowledgeable about the young people of the congregation and community and their issues and concerns, this material can be brought into the morning message. Letting a youth Sunday school class know that the morning message will refer to their mission trip, or something that happened in the local middle school, or someone they know can have a dramatic effect. Many teenagers expect that worship and the morning sermon will contain nothing that relates to their world. If the opposite is true, if they come to worship with the expectation that the person bringing the morning message is likely to refer to something they can relate to, they are more-willing participants.

2. **Use illustrations that relate to the world in which your youth live**. The pastor must speak to the entire congregation. Young people don't expect the pastor to focus exclusively on their concerns every week, but they are as much a part of the congregation as the older members of the church. Illustrative material needs to come from a variety of sources. An illustration that relates to the world youth live in can carry great power—a popular song, a recent movie, a TV show, an event in the community that affects youth, an example from the life of a youth, an example from the pastor's own teenage years—each of these can capture the attention of teenage members of the congregation.

3. **Sing songs that youth enjoy.** Many contemporary denominational hymnals contain songs that young people like and can relate to. In addition, we live in an age in which many organizations are producing CDs and songbooks that contain wonderful new songs that the youth sing at camp and other places. Why not in morning worship? If there is a guitar player (adult or youth) in the congregation, this style of accompaniment can add a whole new dimension to singing and to worship.

   Youth music does not need to replace what the congregation is currently using, but it can supplement it in meaningful ways. Many of the older members of the congregation also enjoy contemporary music. Many of the songs used in youth ministry have been around for nearly thirty years. The baby boomers in the congregation probably know some of these songs as well as the teens do. Other, more recent "praise and worship" music, such as those titles by contemporary artists, can also add much to worship. There are hundreds of new songs that contain wonderful lyrics and are loved by the youth.

4. **Address youth concerns in prayers and liturgy.** There is no reason that the prayers and liturgy used in worship can't address in meaningful ways the issues and concerns of youth. The pastoral prayer can make a reference or two to the

concerns of the younger members of the congregation. A responsive liturgy, affirmation of faith, or prayer of confession can include relevant issues and concerns.

The basic issue in each of these areas is sensitivity—being sensitive to a whole segment of the congregation and attempting to make worship "youth friendly" and relevant to their legitimate concerns and issues.

*"Ever since I was old enough to stay awake through church, the main event for that hour would be counting those who didn't quite make it. 'Big church' is what people call it, simply because it is geared toward the big people or elders of our church. How can we as youth feel a part of the sermon if it is so boring that we end up using the hour as an extension of our Sunday morning sleep? We really could add to the service if we spiced up the youth choir songs by adding a little clapping or motion that would make us feel welcome. If the church were geared toward the family, then all ages would attend; and involvement in the church would grow, including youth."*

Leslie, age 15

## Involving Youth as Leaders

We also can do much to involve young people in the leadership of worship. They have much to offer. With few exceptions, there is nothing an adult can do in worship that a youth cannot also do. They can:

**Serve as Ushers and Greeters.** Many churches have found that young people make excellent ushers. They can greet, hand out bulletins, help seat people, take the offering, and so on. The concern here is the same as it would be with adults—that whoever functions in this role needs to be friendly and have a certain amount of training so that they know what to do.

**Read Scripture.** Many teenagers also make excellent readers. Not every youth can read well, but many do as well as any adult. There will be a certain amount of natural fear the first couple of times a young person (or anyone else) reads before the whole congregation. But this will pass with experience. Help young people get over this fear by having them practice reading aloud the passage from the pulpit before the service.

**Present the Children's Message.** Many young people have an innate ability to relate to younger children. Many have younger brothers and sisters and know how to effectively communicate with children. They may need help with ideas, and an adult may need to sit with them and the children. But in many instances, the chemistry between a youth and the children can enhance the children's message.

**Serve as Liturgists.** If the congregation uses lay liturgists in the morning worship, it would be good to use a young person in this role. There are probably some in most congregations who could do a very effective job of leading prayers, responsive readings, and affirmations of faith.

**Sing in a Youth Choir.** Most adults love it when the youth of the church sing. In some churches, this is done occasionally. In other congregations it is done on a regular basis. If the church has multiple services, the youth might provide music for one of these. If this is the case, it is helpful for the youth choir to be seen occasionally in the other services.

**Serve as Soloists and Musicians.** Many of the youth are trained musicians. They sing in school choirs, perform in orchestras and bands. These are talents that would enhance the Sunday morning worship services for many churches.

**Provide Liturgical Movement or Signing.** Many congregations have come to appreciate and value the contribution that liturgical movement or signing can make to a worship service. Many adults would be intimidated to do this in front of others, but young people often enjoy the opportunity. Youth can sign a prayer, song, or Scripture or do liturgical movement, including sacred dance, for an element of worship. Each of these can provide a powerful and moving addition to the service.

**Serve as Acolytes.** In many congregations, children and teens help with worship by being acolytes. Their duties can include lighting the candles at the beginning of the service, bringing the offering forward, extinguishing the candles at the end of the service, and so on. Junior high students are especially fond of providing this service.

## The Key: Working With the Pastor

The key to involving youth in the morning worship is, and will continue to be, the pastor. In most of our congregations, the responsibility for worship resides with him or her. If we want to involve more young people in worship, we will need to work closely with the pastor.

In my own ministry, I spent twelve years as the pastor in charge before going into full-time youth ministry. As the pastor, I took advantage of a wide variety of opportunities to involve youth in worship. As a member of a church staff, I need to work with the person in charge of worship.

## *Youth Sunday Worship Services*

Even though we can do a lot to make the regular morning worship more youth friendly, much still can be said for occasional "Youth Sunday" worship services. The basic idea for Youth Sunday has been around for a long time. These occasional services are not primarily for the youth. They are services in which the youth of the church—as a group—lead morning worship for the congregation.

There seem to be two basic models of this service currently in use: the "everything but" model and the "total" model. In the "everything but" model, the young people provide everything but the sermon. They sing, read the Scriptures, present the children's message, lead all of the liturgy, prayers, creeds, and so on. Then an adult (the pastor or youth minister) preaches the sermon.

In the "total" model, the young people provide the entire service. Adults help in the planning of the service, but the teenagers lead the service from start to finish, including the sermon. Much can be said for this latter model. Young people have a lot to say. In many of our churches there are youth who can craft and present an excellent sermon. I personally prefer having several share this responsibility. Three or four can collectively speak to a topic or theme. This format takes the pressure off any one youth. If a particular presentation is weak, the others can carry it. The youth can present the morning message in a variety of ways: mini-sermon, personal testimonies, skits, song, and so on.

Another issue to be dealt with is whether to use the regular order of worship. There is a lot to be said for changing the order. A creative tension exists in the unexpected. But for many congregations, following the normal order is easier on both the youth leading and the congregation. If the normal order is followed, different youth simply take the various parts of the service. It is easy to use fifteen to twenty youth in this way. Others can sing in a choir or provide special music.

It's helpful if the youth of the church take on this service as a group and see it as a ministry they are providing to the congregation. Their service needs to be carefully planned and rehearsed. Rehearsing the various parts of the service individually is helpful. You can meet and work with those doing the children's message, the sermon, and the prayers. They may want to stand in the pulpit and practice to get the feel of what they will be doing. An adult can stand at the back of the sanctuary as persons read or speak to see if they can be heard.

It's also helpful to have a dress rehearsal—to run through the service from beginning to end. This lets the participants know whom they follow, what they will do, and who follows them. Rehearsing helps calm fears and performance anxiety and makes the presentation go more smoothly at the service.

## Their Own Worship Service

Even if the youth are actively and meaningfully engaged in the congregation's morning worship and also provide occasional Youth Sunday services for the congregation, they still need opportunities to plan and lead their own services. There is a limit to what worship can do for youth when the focus is on the congregation as a whole.

In most of our churches, the ideal place for a service specifically designed to address the needs and concerns of youth is the Sunday evening youth fellowship. In that setting, the entire worship can be custom-designed for youth and by youth. Both "The Missing *E*" and "The Bracelet" services, mentioned earlier, were created for this setting. Neither of these services could have been presented on Sunday morning, yet each played a crucial role in the life of its respective youth group.

Young people learn more about worship by planning and leading it than they can by sitting in a service. In many youth groups, worship has become a regular part of their time together. Youth fellowship worship services not only are able to address specific needs of the group week after week but also give youth opportunities to plan and lead.

Here is a model with suggestions for a thirty-minute service, planned and led by youth each Sunday. Young people and adults at a senior high summer camp developed the model. It has continued to evolve over the years. Many youth fellowships use this one or one similar as a part of their regular weekly Sunday evening format. It allows for flexibility and creativity, yet its basic structure is simple and consistent.

The model calls for a worship committee (see page 86) of youth and adults who meet before the service and plan the worship. The basic order remains fairly consistent. But the theme and content shifts from week to week, depending upon any needs the worship committee is aware of. Occasionally, the committee will change the usual format of worship for a special service, such as a Catacomb Service or the Lord's Supper.

## *An Order of Worship*

### Gathering

What happens before the service and as it starts is important. If worship is new to the group or if the group has trouble focusing, the members may need to be reminded that they are making a transition from the previous activity to worship. They can be taught an "attitude of worship," or an "attitude of prayer." This attitude involves both reverence for God and respect for the people in the group for whom worship is important and for the sacred space or time they are entering. A musical cue can signal time to get ready for worship.

The setting is also important. If possible, make a physical transition into a different room. If the church sanctuary or chapel is available and helps to create a worshipful atmosphere, use it. If the room leaves something to be desired, turn off the lights and have the service in candlelight. Such changes can have a powerful effect.

Play music as the group enters. A pianist or guitarist can provide music, or use recorded music. Another possibility is to sing the first song as youth enter the room. This will immediately involve the group in the act of worship. Avoid a lull. If there is downtime before the service begins, you may lose the group's attention.

### Opening Songs

Music can set the mood for worship. We usually use three songs. The first is loud and relatively lively. This brings the group on board together. The second song is more moderate. The last is soft and slow and is usually a praise chorus. The cumulative effect is to have the group focus together and then slowly calm down. If your group already has reverence for worship, you may want to use only mellow songs.

Use young people as song leaders. Volunteers who are not part of the leadership team can lead the music. If possible, have different people in this role each week.

### Opening Prayer

Ask one of the youth to open with prayer. This should be short and, if possible, introduce the theme of the worship service. You might want to use some of the prayer forms mentioned in Chapter 2, such as the responsive prayers.

### Scripture Presentation

Ask an individual or a group to present the Scripture. Reading is only one way to present a Scripture passage. It can be acted out, mimed, paraphrased, reverse paraphrased, and so on. If the passage is short, reading it may be best. If it is a story, a dramatic presentation of the text might be appropriate. Variety is helpful. Teenagers are more inclined to listen to the passage if the approaches vary from week to week.

### The Devotion

The devotion, or the "message" part of the service, can be presented in a wide variety of ways: through testimonies, having one or more persons say what the passage means to them, or through dramas or skits. The speaker can also draw from books of devotions and adapt the selections. The most powerful devotions, though, are the ones created by the group for a specific situation, such as the "The Missing *E*" and "The Bracelet," mentioned earlier (page 73).

## Response

Don't limit the presentation of the message to the worship leadership team. Following the message, open up the meeting to the group as a whole and invite comments and thoughts. At times, no one will have anything to add. At other times, the most powerful words spoken may be by someone in the group.

## Joys and Concerns

Invite the group to a time of telling of joys, concerns, and prayer requests. One person can introduce this to the group and suggest a sentence to be said after each concern is voiced. You might want to use "Hear our prayer, O Lord," or "This is our prayer," or some other appropriate form. This response lets the group know when one concern is over and it is OK to give the next. It's also helpful if the person leading the joys and concerns will repeat each joy or concern first, as in, "A concern for Tim's mother, who is in the hospital. Hear our prayer, O Lord." This pattern helps make sure that everyone hears each concern.

## Altar Prayer Time or the Lord's Prayer

In many of our churches, we lost the opportunity to pray at the altar rail when we lost our evening services. Many young people find a time of silent prayer at the altar rail to be especially valuable. After the concerns, joys, and prayer requests have been voiced, ask the leader to invite the group to come to the altar for a time of prayer. Dim the lights if you have not already done so. If possible, have soft music (taped or live) playing in the background. Don't rush this part of the service, but encourage the group members to take the time they need.

*"For me, worship is one of the most important parts of my spirituality. It is a time when I can focus solely on God and my faith. The part of worship that is the most meaningful to me is altar time. My prayers at the altar seem to be more inspired and more directed. It's as if I'm connected to God through the songs, prayers, and Scriptures of the worship. Sharing a worship experience with others helps me feel enlightened in the Holy Spirit, therefore my prayer at the altar reflects the love and fulfillment I have experienced in worship."*

Nicole, age 16

An alternative to ending the joys and concerns with altar prayer time is to simply close by asking the group to recite the Lord's Prayer. This allows the group members to end the prayer time as a group and clearly signals that prayer time is over and the next part of the service is about to begin.

## Closing Circle (Prayer, Song, Benediction)

When the group has finished praying, ask the members to form a circle by linking arms. In large groups, you may want them to form rows or simply reach out on either side for someone's hand. The ritual of the closing circle becomes very meaningful to the group. It can have three parts: A youth can close with a brief prayer. The group can sing a short, simple song that everyone knows. Then the group can end with a benediction:

[24] The LORD bless you and keep you;
[25] the LORD make his face to shine upon you, and be gracious to you;
[26] the LORD lift up his countenance upon you, and give you peace.

(Numbers 6:24-26)

Some youth groups vary this benediction by accentuating the word *you,* or by looking at a different person each time the word *you* is said, or by pointing to a different person each time. Encourage the group to "get some hugs" after the service.

## *Creating a Devotional*

Even though there are available numerous devotional books with meditations that can be adapted for youth worship, the best devotions are those that the group creates for the situation. Here is a simple process for preparing ones that are both biblically faithful and appropriate to the situation. This formula was developed in the summer camp setting. It uses the following steps:

1. **Exegete the passage.** It's easy to proof-text Scripture. Young people find it easy to have some point they want to communicate and then ask for some Scripture to back it up. The trouble is that this is *isogesis*—reading into the Scripture what we want it to say. This approach does violence to the Scripture and is inappropriate for Christian worship.

   A better approach is *exegesis*—to read out of the text what it is saying. This is relatively simple for most passages of Scripture. An adult can help a group of youth

   a. read the passage
   b. decide what its theme or topic is
   c. then decide what it says about the topic

   These steps are the starting point for the service. Everything else is built on what we understand the Scripture to be saying, not vice versa.

2. **Exegete the group.** The next step is to exegete the group, much as you did the passage:

   • What is going on in our group right now?
   • What are the issues and concerns with which we are struggling?
   • Where do the issues of our group meet the issues raised by the Scripture?

   At times, a group may want to reverse the first two steps in order to consider a particular issue with which the group is dealing. In this case, the group might want to examine what is going on in the group and determine the issue. Then the group can look for appropriate Scriptures that deal with the same or related issues. If the steps are reversed, it is important to make sure that the texts found are used for what they really say, not for what the group wants them to say.

3. **Decide what to say to the group.** Decide based on what this passage says to this group at this time. Three concerns are central here:

   a. the message will be based on the Scripture
   b. it is appropriate to the group to whom it is being presented
   c. it is appropriate to that moment

4. **Decide how you will present it.** Once you have decided what it is you want to say, based on the first three steps, you can decide how you will communicate this message. You may want to use a skit, testimonies, an idea from a book. Once you know where you're going, it is relatively easy to decide how to get there.

5. **Decide who will do or say it.** This step is the one that many young people want to take first. The problem is that if several people have strong opinions about wanting to do particular things before the group decides—as a group—what it wants to do, there is a danger that the worship will be ill focused. Worship is not a showcase for individual talents. Our talents are subservient to the service itself. Having this step follow the previous four steps guarantees that when a person volunteers to lead the worship, he or she will lead the worship that the committee has planned.

6. **Plan the rest of the service around this message.** Once the devotion is planned, the rest of the service follows quickly and naturally. The planners can choose or create prayers, songs, and other elements to fit the devotion and the theme.

## *Communion*

Communion, the Lord's Supper, needs to be a regular part of youth worship. Unfortunately, most youth groups do not have an ordained person working with the group. But serving Holy Communion is an excellent opportunity to involve the pastor. Also, in the typical youth group, there are people who are not members of the church or who may not come on Sunday morning. Regular, monthly Communion allows the sacrament to be a part of the life of the group and the pastor to connect with the youth in a meaningful and appropriate way.

## *Worship on Trips and Special Occasions*

Worshiping together at camp or on a trip or retreat is a practice that becomes an important part of the shared experience. Camps and retreats are often held in beautiful natural settings. A vespers service at sunset can set a wonderful mood for worship. Worship times can be brief and yet satisfying as they bring the whole group together as a community of faith.

Because young people are open to new ideas, they can also be a conduit for introducing new and exciting worship experiences into the congregation. Adults expect the youth to do things that are different. The worshiping congregation is more tolerant when the youth do new and innovative things than it often is of the pastor doing so.

Special occasions provide wonderful opportunities for the youth to lead the entire congregation in worship. Many congregations find the following times especially appropriate for youth leadership:

## 1. Easter Sunrise Service

In countless congregations, the youth of the church provide the Easter sunrise service. The youth can plan and lead the service, which can then be followed by a fellowship time, with breakfast at the church or a local restaurant. The youth choir can sing songs; youth can perform skits; youth can give testimonies. The service can be brief, but is best if it begins in twilight and reaches its climax just as the sun cracks over the horizon.

## 2. Good Friday Tenebrae Service

The Good Friday Tenebrae service is built around a series of readings that retell the story of the last night in the life of Jesus. Many churches have discovered that the youth of the church can provide the readers and the music for this service. Tenebrae is a kind of reverse candlelight service that has a lot of emotional power and can focus the congregation's attention on the meaning of Lent.

## 3. Contemporary Hymn Sing

Young people are often the first to learn contemporary Christian music. Many of the songs they sing on retreats, at camps, and at their evening fellowship are songs the congregation would also appreciate. The baby-boomers and younger generations were raised on many of the same songs. The youth could introduce these songs into morning worship or—on special occasions—provide a contemporary hymn sing.

## 4. Praise Worship Service

Many young people are familiar with contemporary praise worship. They experience this form of worship at summer camps, at youth events, at Young Life, and in a wide variety of settings. With or without a band, youth and their leaders are fully capable of providing a worship experience that many people of all ages find extremely attractive and meaningful.

## 5. Catacomb Worship

Catacomb worship is an emotionally powerful form of worship that has become popular in recent years. This service recreates what it was like to worship in the early Christian community. There were no Bibles or songbooks. Often, the leaders of the community were in prison or had been killed. The idea played out in the catacomb experience is that we—our memories, our experiences, our faith—are the basic resource for worship. *The Catacomb Project: Hope for 2000 and Beyond,* by Samuel F. Parvin, et al. (Abingdon Press, 1999; ISBN 0687074916), gives a fuller picture of this unique experience.

- The catacomb service is a candlelight service.
- Find a room that the group can fit into but in which they will be cramped.
- Use votive candles to form a cross on the floor in the center of the room.
- As the group enters the room, have someone start a song the group knows.

- As each song ends, someone else starts another or calls out the title of a song so that another person can start it. The group sings as much of each song as it remembers, and can sing as long as it wants.
- Then someone asks if a person present will lead the opening prayer. Do the same for joys and concerns.

When it is time to read Scripture, the leader mentions that there are no Bibles and invites people to recite Scripture passages that are important to them. The Scripture can be quoted exactly or summarized. Someone may just remember a story in brief form.

After the Scripture, someone invites the people to tell what they think God might say to this group at this moment. Anyone who wants to contribute does so. If possible, the group then has Communion, singing softly in the background as the elements are served. Worship ends with a closing prayer, and everyone departs the room in silence.

Two things are important in doing a catacomb service. Although it appears that the service is leaderless, make sure that people who know what is supposed to happen are ready to facilitate. Individuals need to be prepared to start songs, give prayer requests, Scripture passages, and the Word of the Lord. No one wants to be first in any of these; but if a few can break the ice, the whole group will often follow. One or more facilitators need to be ready to ask people to pray or add their witness at appropriate times.

Another thing that is important for a catacomb service is to carefully explain to the group members before they enter the room what you are doing and how it will work. Set expectations high. The more seriously the youth take the service, the more they will get out of it.

### 6. A Message-less Prayer Service

A message-less service follows the same order as the youth fellowship worship model, mentioned above, except that there will be no devotion or message. Prayer becomes the focus of the service. The group sings, tells joys and concerns, has altar prayer time, then closes. This form of worship is especially appropriate when time is limited, when someone forgets to plan the service, or when a break is needed from the regular order.

## *The Worship Committee*

A youth worship committee planned many of the worship services mentioned in this chapter. Worship doesn't just happen. It needs to be carefully planned and led by the youth. One of the best ways to accomplish this on a regular basis is to have a standing worship committee. It may be a part of your youth council structure or exist separately.

Many churches have a representative from each grade and adult volunteers form the group that is responsible for seeing that worship is planned. In a small church two youth and one adult could take on the task. The committee members are not to lead all the worship services themselves. Their responsibility is twofold:

1. to plan worship
2. to recruit others to help them lead the worship experiences

The adult acts as a facilitator or enabler. The adult keeps the process on track and helps the group think through what it wants to say. The young people provide the basic ideas and the up-front leadership. The adult can be instrumental in giving support, sparking ideas, and helping the group prepare for the service.

Worship is central to spiritual growth. Young people need to be included in the worship of the congregation. Yet they also need opportunities to create their own services that focus on their needs. I hope that this chapter has given you some ideas that you can use with your group as you develop its spirituality in worship.

# SMALL GROUPS

CHAPTER

**I**n the summer of 1982, I was a small-group leader at a high school camp. As I led the group and encouraged members to talk openly and honestly about what was going on in their lives, they did just that. They began to tell of their pain, their struggles, their deepest life issues.

I listened to young people talk about what they had never told anyone else. They were saying things they desperately needed to say. They said things they had been unable to say because they had never before found a place to say them and people to listen. The experience was one of the most moving of my life. I felt the presence of God in a way I had not before.

That conversation changed the direction of my ministry and led to the book *Sharing Groups in Youth Ministry* (Abingdon Press, 1991). That book focused on small groups as part of a caring ministry. Since then, the small-group movement, in various styles, has exploded in popularity. Churches are recognizing the role and value of small groups in Christian formation.

Relationship lies at the heart of the Christian faith. We are called into a dynamic, living relationship with God, not just an understanding of God. Jesus' dual commandment is the norm: We are called to love God and neighbor, to be in relationship with the living God, and to be in relationship with those around us. "On these two commandments," according to Jesus, "hang all the law and the prophets" (Matthew 22:40). Relationship is primary; all else is secondary. We're not called to just learn *about* God, but to be in relationship *with* the living God.

## *Why Small Groups?*

Small-group ministry based on relationships. One could argue that a small group is a lab in Christian relationships and Christian living.

Small groups help youth experience community and intimacy and give them a safe place to explore their faith. A small group is an optimal environment for the life change Jesus Christ intends for every believer—connecting people to one another and to God. Our theological task as leaders is to help youth mature, to help them grow in faith and become all that God wants them to be. Small groups play a vital role in spiritual growth and spiritual formation.

Some churches call their small groups "cells." If the church is the "body" of Christ, then small groups are the cells of the body, the places where the body functions at its most basic level. Likewise, a small group can be seen as the basic functional unit of the Christian life. The church gathers as a corporate body for worship. It serves God in the world. But it is fed, nurtured, and lives out its life in the small-group environment.

This thinking has been reflected in the emergence of cell churches and cell movements. In these movements an even greater transition has been made. The question is asked: Does a local church congregation "have" small groups as a part of its ministry; or, as these movements advocate, is the local congregation actually constituted and made up of cells—intentional small groups?

The small group is an excellent place for intentional, in-depth discipling of people. Many believe that it is the best place to grow spiritually. The intimate, personal, and accountable nature of the small group is ideal for spiritual growth and growth in discipleship.

*"Being in small groups has had an affect on me, because the pressures of 'pretending you don't care' go away. In Sunday school, the majority of the class carries on private conversation during the lesson; whereas in small group, everyone settles down and takes the topic to heart. In large groups, people tend to lose interest and miss the message entirely; while others who have a desire to learn are distracted by the constant stirring of the person beside them. I have found that small groups provide a more friendly atmosphere, and that it is easier to pour out your heart and share feelings with a group who knows you and respects your beliefs."*

John, age 16

There is a historic link between spiritual growth and the intensive small-group experience. John Wesley organized the early Methodists into classes. Young Life, Campus Crusade, and other groups that are intentional about spiritual growth and discipleship have used the small group as one of their primary tools. In recent times, entire congregations, such as Willow Creek, have been organized around the small-group paradigm.

Small groups serve many functions. Many of the basic needs of youth can be met in the small-group setting. Some of these are spiritual, some are psychological, and some fall into other categories. Whenever we have youth in small groups, any or all of these factors may be at play:

- The need to have a safe place to talk about ideas, feelings, experiences.
- The need to be with peers and friends and to find a place of acceptance with them.
- The need to belong to a group, to have fellowship with others.
- The need for intimacy, to know and be known at a deeply personal level.
- The need to have a sounding board for values, beliefs, ideas, and feelings, and a safe environment to try out new things.
- The need to find answers to important life questions.
- The need for spiritual growth, to be fed at a spiritual level and encouraged to grow in faith.
- The need for significant adult relationships.
- The need to know what others think and value and why they hold these views.
- The need for a positive model for building healthy relationships.

## *Types of Small Groups*

Contemporary youth ministry makes heavy use of small groups for a variety of reasons, including intentional spiritual growth. Several models and variations exist:

### Covenant Discipleship Groups

Covenant discipleship groups agree to meet weekly and hold one another accountable for their spiritual disciplines. They agree together to read the Bible, pray, attend worship, and participate in a variety of spiritual disciplines. The Upper Room has materials available for setting up and running such groups. See the website www.upperroom.org/fivecircles/walking.asp and the book *Guide for Covenant Discipleship Groups*.

### Spiritual Growth Groups

Spiritual growth groups focus less on holding one another accountable for specific spiritual disciplines and more on giving one another support with the question, "How goes it with your spirit?" Some groups resemble discussion groups and may work through a book together. Others focus on Bible study. Some are more of a spiritual support group and deal with personal issues and their effect on our spiritual walk.

### Student-Led Small Groups

Especially with senior high youth, student-led small groups are increasingly popular. Meeting usually in homes during the week, they are often centered around Bible study. Two youth share leadership; an adult in the group acts as an encourager behind the scenes. The youth invite their friends; the groups grow and split after reaching ten to twelve. Then they grow again. The small group environment is conducive to helping both committed youth and their seeker friends grow spiritually. For more information about these groups, visit *www.ileadyouth.com*.

### Sharing Groups

Sharing groups are support groups that deal specifically with personal emotional issues. But these groups lend themselves readily to spiritual growth concerns. A sharing group made up of church members and meeting at the church will include, as one of its natural components, the spiritual lives of the members.

## *Ensuring Small-Group Success*

Every small group has at least two elements. The first is some specific task. For some it is Bible study; for others, support. For some it is being accountable for spiritual disciplines and the Christian life; for others it is reaching new youth and helping both committed and seeker youth grow as disciples. The task might center around a particular concern (getting along with parents) or an activity (learning to play music together). It may involve a one-shot small group that meets at youth fellowship. It may require an ongoing small group in the Sunday school setting or at another time during the week. In any case, each small group has an agenda, a curriculum, some content it is trying to communicate.

Regardless of the task, all small groups are also about relationships. Whatever the content we are teaching, our ultimate goal is to connect people relationally, shaping the young persons into the image God desires for them. Whatever task we are doing, whatever content we are teaching, relationships are at the center of our goal of Christian spiritual formation.

Neither of the two elements is accomplished automatically. Several factors will affect the life of the group and its ability to perform the functions we intend for it. Those factors can be addressed and controlled to best serve the group.

## Group Size

An ideal group size for discussion is about five to seven persons. If the group has more than ten people present, it is best to divide the youth into two smaller groups. A group that has fewer than five members may not contain within itself sufficient personal experiences or resources to produce meaningful dialogue. The cell-group model allows for groups to grow, divide, and grow again. (See "Student-Led Groups," page 91.)

## Group Acceptance and Respect

In the most supportive and effective groups, each member of the group accepts every other member as a person of worth, leaving no one feeling rejected or not desired in that group. A group needs to be open to differences of all kinds. Suppressing any conflicts or differences in ideas or opinions will hurt the functional level of the group.

## Learning to Listen

In strong groups, the members learn to listen to one another. They create an atmosphere in which each person has an equal opportunity to participate in the life and discussion of the group. When participants feel listened to, the conversation will flow easily back and forth; ideas and opinions are freely expressed and heard.

## Freedom of Expression

Members can learn to understand the feelings of others and show respect for others, whether or not they agree with them. Group members can be encouraged to freely participate and welcome a diversity of opinions, including opinions that are different from those they personally hold or even opinions that are different from what the group holds. Confidentiality is appropriately observed.

## Group Covenants

One way to ensure the success of a group is to begin with certain commitments. The members can covenant together to keep those commitments. They may need to be reminded of these basic guidelines from time to time. Here is a sample of a covenant:

1. **Take ownership of the group and the discussion.** Group members need to remember that it is our discussion—yours and mine. Together we can make it good or make it bad.

2. **Learn to listen.** A discussion is different from several monologues. We need to hear what the other is saying before we respond.

3. **Respect the person speaking.** We need to show that respect even if we disagree with that person's ideas or values. Then, and only then, do we have the right to expect others to respect our views, opinions, thoughts, and values.

4. **Check it out.** When in doubt, make sure you understand what the other person is saying before you respond. Ask: "Are you saying that. . . ."

5. **Let others know.** Let others know your thoughts, your ideas, your opinions, your feelings. Don't keep them to yourself. We want and need to hear your contribution to the group life.

6. **Let others carry the ball too.** Don't dominate the discussion. Contribute to the discussion without dominating it. Discussion is give and take, talking and listening.

7. **Stick to the point.** Stay on the subject. And allow us to remind you if you have wandered away from what we were talking about.

8. **Keep the conversation here.** Don't talk to people outside the group about what people in the group have said or done. Make this group a safe place for being oneself and dealing honestly with the issues of our lives.

## *The Role of the Small-Group Leader*

If the small group is to create an environment for Christian discipleship, the most strategic person is the leader or facilitator. Small groups do not work without leadership. In much of the recent literature on Christian growth groups, the role of the leader or facilitator takes up most of the space.

The leader or facilitator ensures that the group works. The leader initiates activities and provides a sense of purpose and vision. The facilitator takes responsibility for the small-group process and makes sure that the group environment is safe and nonthreatening. The leader or facilitator defines group expectations, sets boundaries, and encourages group members.

## Attending

Whether the small-group task centers on personal caring, Bible study, or some activity, listening can be the most important factor in the group relationship. If we who are in the role of leader or facilitator do not listen to group members, then we will not be able to help them.

Small groups will benefit from an intentional type of listening, called "active listening" or "empathy." Both terms describe a process in which we deliberately attend to what a person is saying and then let the person know what we have heard.

The first step in active listening is attending—paying attention to what is being said. Not everything a person says is of equal importance; much of the conversation is filler, extra details, and extraneous material. As young people talk to us in a group, we can sort through what they are saying to glean what is important to them.

Sometimes the gleaning requires reading between the lines. There is more to what a person says than just "content." Attending is listening in such a way that we understand what is being said (the content) and how the person feels about it (the affect).

## Acknowledging

After we pay careful attention to what the person says, the second step in active listening is communicating what we have heard. We must let the youth know that we have heard them—that we have heard both the content (what they have said) and the affect (how they feel about it).

Wee need not agree with what is said; it is important to acknowledge that we hear and understand. We should neither take away from nor add to what someone is saying. The idea behind active listening is to reflect what the person has said to us as accurately as possible. This step lets the person know that we're listening, that we're taking the time and the effort to pay attention to what he or she is saying. Not only does this step acknowledge that what was said was heard, it also acknowledges the worth of the speaker.

Active listening is a skill. It is learned through practice. At first the practice may seem awkward and artificial; but with time and experience, it will become easy. Most young people have a deep need to be heard—to be really heard. If we can provide youth with a place and a relationship in which they can be heard, then we are taking the first step in helping them.

## Asking Good Questions

In addition to attending and acknowledging, asking questions effectively can become a significant factor in the relational effectiveness of a small group. In general, questions are either closed ended (can be answered with a quick yes or no or some other quick response) or they are open ended (they invite the person to say more). Questions are also either content oriented or affect (feeling) oriented.

In general, open-ended, affective questions invite the most openness; but they are also the most psychologically threatening. Closed and content questions are best to begin the discussion, then these can be followed by deeper questions.

## *Twenty Techniques to Trigger Great Discussion*

Many of the most effective small-group strategies and activities can be found in other chapters of this book. Most Bible study ideas work well in small groups. Listening prayers and spoken prayers can take on profound new elements when experienced in a small group. The following ideas work particularly well as ways to encourage interaction and to generate discussion. Some are for especially helpful for short-term or quick groupings within the larger group.

### 1. Powerball

Provide a ball of any size. Have the group form a circle. Whoever has the ball has the "power"—the power to talk. Whoever has the ball has to talk. This person also has the power to decide who speaks next by giving him or her the ball.

### 2. Insider/Outsider

Those who have something to say or contribute sit on the inside circle and talk with one another. The rest of the group sits on the outside in a second circle, listening. Reverse roles.

### 3. Values Clarification

Have individuals stand in a continuum, based on how they feel (or think) about a particular issue.

### 4. Fox Holes

In a large group meeting, "fox holes" or "break-out" groups of five to six youth can help build community. If possible, have each team include an adult.

### 5. Small Group Assignments

As needed, assign persons a specific job or task to do during the discussion—facilitator, reader, recorder, reporter, or timekeeper.

### 6. Jig Saw

Let youth form their own groups of three or four persons (with their friends). Then have them number off within each group (1, 2, 3, [4], 1, 2, 3, [4], and so forth). Have the *1*s form a group, the *2*s form a group, and so forth. Give each of these groups a different assignment (Scripture or topic to discuss). After the discussion, have them reassemble in their original groups. Each person is to tell his or her group what was discussed in the number group.

### 7. Dyads and Triads

Divide into groups of two or three to discuss thoughts or feelings on an issue. In groups of three, one of the members can be an observer, who reports on the process as a whole.

### 8. Task Groups

In a larger group, give smaller groups a different task or assignment to complete. The groups then report to the total class what they discovered.

## 9. Skits

Have the group or members of the group create a brief skit that raises an issue that you (or they) want to discuss. Several small groups could do different skits.

## 10. Debate

Have the group conduct a formal (or semiformal) debate on an issue, using this process: 1) formulate a stance or position, 2) state the position, 3) rebut the other team's position, 4) close the argument. Important: Don't vote at the end. Instead, let the debate lead into a discussion.

## 11. Yarn Discussion

Have someone tie the loose end of a ball of yarn around his or her wrist and then throw the ball to the person whom they want to speak next. That person holds on to the yarn as he or she speaks and continues to hold the yarn while throwing the ball to another person. Each person, in turn, does the same as the discussion progresses. Note who has not spoken. Note who has. Have the group express feelings or attitudes through the woven web.

## 12. Devil's Advocate

Play the part of the devil's advocate. Deliberately take the opposite view from the majority or a view that is provocative in order to stimulate discussion on a topic. For example, say, "There is no God, and you can't convince me that there is one."

## 13. Research Groups

Have smaller groups do research into a topic or topics. Then have them report their findings to the others.

## 14. "I Heard You Say" Discussion

In this discussion, each person has to complete the sentence "I heard you say . . ." to the person to whom he or she is responding—and to the satisfaction of that person. Once the person has agreed that the listener has correctly heard and understood what he or she said, only then can the listener make a comment.

## 15. Reverse Debate

This technique is the same as a regular debate but with a twist. Have the teams divide up on an issue, and let each side take the position they actually hold (or want to argue for) in the debate. Then switch them and require them to take the opposite side of the issue.

## 16. Newspaper Skits

Bring in a stack of newspapers and rolls of masking tape. Have groups create skits, using only props and costumes made from newspapers and masking tape.

## 17. Grab Bag Skits

Gather enough bags for each small group to have one. Each bag should contain a half dozen items—completely unrelated and randomly selected. Each small group is to create a skit on the topic you give them, using every item in the grab bag and using every member of the group.

## 18. On Site Field Trips

Studying mission? Take a field trip and do something for mission. Think of places and activities that would enhance the topic you are studying or discussing. An excellent resource for small groups is *Destination Unknown: 50 Quick Mystery Trips for Youth Groups,* by Sam Halverson (Abingdon Press, 2001; ISBN 068709724X). On a "DU," the members do not know where they are going (parents do, however). When the group arrives at the mystery site, which is related to a biblical passage or theme, the discussion is quite lively—and memorable.

## 19. Games That Relate to the Issue

Think of existing games (or ones you can make up) that relate to the issue you want to discuss. Play the game as a way of stimulating discussion.

## 20. Challenge Games and Activities

There are hundreds of these: trust walks, trust falls, 4-ball teamwork exercise, Chocolate River, Electric Fence, Spider Web. Think of something you want to discuss; there is probably an exercise that will help provoke discussion. The book, *Go For It! Games: 25 Faith-Building Adventures for Groups,* by Walt Marcum (Abingdon Press, 1998; ISBN 0687087287) provides not only the exercises but also Scripture connections and discussion questions.

# SPECIAL TECHNIQUES AND RESOURCES

**B**ible study, prayer, and worship have long been the core tools for spiritual growth. This fact has remained unchanged for several thousand years and is likely to remain unchanged. But these three are not the only available tools for spiritual growth. There are a lot of different ways to foster spiritual formation. This chapter will briefly explore some of these techniques and resources. Books have been written on most of these topics. The concern here is to note how each of these techniques can be used to enhance our relationship with God and our spiritual growth.

## *Spiritual Mentoring*

In a sense, any adult who works with youth is a spiritual mentor. Young people naturally look up to the adults who work with them as role models and mentors. No matter what the official task of the mentor and youth, the relationship is likely to contribute to spiritual growth. to some degree. However, the term, *spiritual mentoring* has a more restricted meaning.

Through the ages, Christians who have wanted to grow in their faith have sought out others to help in their spiritual journey. Among peers, these are often referred to as spiritual friends, friends in faith, or what Morton Kelsey has called "companions on the inner way."

A spiritual mentor is an adult who agrees to work with one or more youth on a one-to-one basis. The content of the meetings is the spiritual journey. The mentor helps the young person by asking the age-old question, "How goes it with your spirit?" This approach is sometimes called spiritual counseling or spiritual direction. It is similar to a counseling relationship, except that the content is explicitly spiritual, rather than psychological; and the purpose is to enhance the relationship, rather than to troubleshoot a problem.

The mentor and the student can process Scripture, work through a book, discuss life experiences, explore issues, or do whatever seems appropriate to the relationship. Preparing for confirmation has become a key time for spiritual mentoring. Both United Methodists and Lutheran confirmation materials have resources specifically to help young persons talk about their faith.

In the broader sense, we have this relationship with each youth with whom we work. Or looking at it from the other direction, a youth should be able to see each of the adults who work with the youth program as a spiritual mentor. Being intentional about this aspect of our relationship can enhance our ministry to young people.

## *Journaling*

Journaling is a way to keep a record of our relationship with God and our journey of faith. It involves writing down one's thoughts, feelings, and experiences in relation to God and our walk with God, our discipleship. Journaling has already been discussed as a prayer technique, but it also can be used as a spiritual growth tool. Within youth ministry, three approaches to journaling are particularly helpful:

### 1. The Diary Approach

In the diary approach, the person keeping the spiritual journal writes entries, just as one would in a diary. The difference is in the content of the diary. Instead of being random thoughts and feelings or a log of the day's experiences, the journal keeper focuses on those things that seem to have some relationship to his or her spiritual journey.

### 2. Letters to God

The journal keeper may want to write letters to God in a "Dear Abby" fashion. Instead of writing to a columnist for advice, the letters are written to God. In this way, the writer is free to pour out his or her inner thoughts and feelings and lift them to God in prayer form.

### 3. Dialogues With God

The journal keeper may want to enter into a dialogue with God in written form. The writer would write "Dear Abby" type entries then add what he or she believes that God would say in reply.

In the following chapter on retreats, you will find several examples of journaling used as a spiritual growth tool.

## *Spiritual Autobiographies*

We usually do not take time to stop and reflect on the presence of God in our lives and our spiritual journeys. The purpose of a spiritual autobiography is to take a look at our lives and see where God has had an effect. This takes the idea popularized by the "Footprints" poem, which seems to find its way onto posters with each succeeding group of youth, and expands it. In a spiritual autobiography, a person may write on such topics as:

1. My earliest awareness or experience of God
2. The moment I felt closest to God
3. The time when God felt most real
4. A time when I felt distant from God
5. Important events that have shaped my faith
6. Important people in my spiritual formation
7. Where I am right now in my relationship with God
8. One thing missing in my relationship with God is. . . .
9. Struggles I have in my faith or my walk with God

Chapter 7 includes an example of a spiritual autobiography (page 124). In addition to writing responses to various topics, there are several other inventive ways to create spiritual autobiographies that work well with youth.

## 1. Written Autobiography

One alternative is to write your life story in paragraph form, focusing on the issues that have affected your relationship with God and your spiritual journey. The nine topics above, and others like them, can be used to guide the writer.

## 2. Life Graph

For those who are more visual, a life graph is a possibility. A life graph looks like an electrocardiogram or an EEG, with a jagged line going up and down. The person making the graph draws his or her life, with all its ups and downs then goes back and adds words or symbols to note particular events or people. In this form, both the personal life and the spiritual life of the person are shown at the same time. After the graph is completed, the person can tell the class or a group about his or her spiritual journey, using the graph as an aid.

## 3. Dual Graph

A dual graph is similar to the graph above, with one exception. Two graphs are created, one on top of the other. One graph narrates the person's personal life. The other narrates the spiritual journey. The dual graph is especially helpful in showing how our personal lives affect our spiritual journeys and vice versa.

## 4. Road Map

Junior high or middle school students are especially fond of the road map approach. In this approach, a person's life is depicted as a road, with dead ends, under-construction signs, accidents, potholes, and hazards. The pictorial possibilities are wonderful.

### 5. Pipe-cleaner Graph

Junior high and middle school youth also can use a pipe cleaner (or chenille stem) to make a graph. By bending the wire up and down, they can depict the highs and lows of the spiritual journey. In this approach, nothing is usually written down. The young person simply explains what the ups and downs on the wire mean. Using the pipe-cleaner graph will usually result in less content and a shorter amount of explaining, but its advantage is that it is quick, easy, and can be done on the spur of the moment.

The key to all of these approaches is interpretation, rather than presentation. The spiritual autobiography becomes a means of opening up. The presentation of the graph and the discussion that follows are what is important. In small groups, group members may ask questions about the autobiography. The group gains a better understanding of the person and can help the presenter see things that he or she may otherwise have missed.

## *Dream Work*

Throughout the history of our faith, dreams have been seen as one of the ways in which God speaks to us. Even in a psychological approach, it is clear that our dreams are important and can help us understand what is going on in our lives. Dreams that have religious symbolism or seem to convey something important can be truly relevant to our walk with God. Taking the time to understand a dream, whether in a personal journal or in a small group setting, can be helpful.

In the bibliography, you will find listed the book, *Dreams and Spiritual Growth: A Christian Approach to Dreamwork,* by Louis M. Savary, et al.,which contains more than thirty dreamwork approaches helpful in understanding the religious significance of dreams.

## *Music*

Music has the power to speak to the soul. It is not accidental that music is a crucial part of worship. Young people also find music and singing powerful spiritual disciplines, in and of themselves. Music ties directly to the emotions. It has the power to evoke memories. Music and group singing should be a vital part of any youth program. Many excellent music resources are available.

*Cokesbury Chorus Book, Expanded Edition, Praise and Worship Music for Today's Church* (Abingdon Press, 1999; ISBN 068707028) includes choruses popular with youth today. In addition, you will find numerous CDs with songbooks that are being published with contemporary songs.

Most of these songs have a few simple chords, and one strumming pattern works for nearly all of them. It is not unusual for a youth to learn in a few weeks how to play the guitar well enough to lead group singing. Listening to music, having music as background for prayer time or singing together will add a dimension to youth worship and to the spiritual tone of group gatherings.

## *Fasting*

Fasting has been called "the forgotten discipline" and is rarely discussed in youth circles, although some groups will have an Easter vigil fast or a fast on New Year's Eve. Historically, fasting serves several purposes. Some youth leaders use fasting to heighten sensitivity to world hunger and poverty issues. Others have used it as a tool for self-denial and discipline. But the original purpose of fasting was quite different. Fasting was originally linked to prayer, especially meditation and contemplation. Those who fast claim that it clears the mind so that they can focus more intently. There is some evidence that fasting causes biochemical changes in the body.

In youth work, fasting needs to be used with great care. Youth bodies are developing and are growing rapidly. They have special nutritional needs. The literature on fasting recommends that youth never fast longer than twenty-four hours and that they be allowed to drink fluids (especially juice). For spiritual growth, it is also important to debrief the experience.

If fasting is used as a tool for spiritual growth, it needs to be used for a purpose; and the purpose needs to be clearly stated. Otherwise, young people will not understand the difference between a spiritual fast and dieting to lose weight.

## *Depth Discipleship Training*

A common complaint by many young people is that they are not challenged. Sunday school is "boring." They are not learning anything new. The list goes on and on. Although we need a healthy skepticism about some of these statements, we also need to listen to the concern behind the words. Many youth are not sufficiently challenged by the ministry we currently offer them; they are ready for more. This desire will probably not be true for all the youth in your church, or even the majority; but it will be true for some.

We need to provide challenging, depth experiences for these young people. They are ready for intentional discipleship training. Here we are not looking for numbers. We are not seeking to sell the idea so that we can attract as many people as possible. Depth training, such as the youth edition of DISCIPLE, Covenant Discipleship groups, peer counseling, or Chrysalis weekends, can be offered to those who are ready and have expressed an interest. Groups need to be small so that each person can have individual attention. These groups also need to be long term. It takes time to work through spiritual growth issues or to take a youth to a new level of spiritual growth.

In addition to the programs available that provide opportunities for depth discipleship training, you may want to create your own study or format.

Recently in our church, we created a new Sunday school class for senior high youth who felt that they were not challenged by the traditional classes. They requested a class where the answers were not assumed, where they could ask difficult theological questions, such as "How do I really know that there is a God?" "How do I really know that anything I am taught about our faith is true?" "What really makes Jesus better than Mohammed or Buddha?" They were asking for what in seminary is called "systematic theology."

We created the new class, hoping that the three or four who had requested it (and perhaps a few more) would be motivated enough to attend on a regular basis. Much to everyone's surprise, we have been averaging thirty youth each Sunday. The class members are even bringing their friends from high school to attend the class.

Most of our groups contain youth who need more, who need to dig deeper into the faith. Some of these will approach this from the skeptical side, while others will approach it from the opposite direction. When this type of training is reserved for the leadership "core group," we make a mistake. Those who are ready for depth training and those who have the inclination and the ability to be leaders may or may not be the same people.

One of the special issues that arises in the midst of youth ministry, especially with depth discipleship training, is the question of how to handle calls to ministry. It is a privilege to be there with young people when this issue arises. If we are uncomfortable with the topic or feel that it raises issues with which we are not adequately trained to deal, we can request the assistance of the pastor or someone else on the church staff.

Our role is to neither push nor hinder but to gently encourage the young person to work through his or her feelings and thoughts. If the young person feels called by God to professional ministry, we can affirm the call without burdening the young person with the thought that this decision is for life. The call may take a new direction in the future, or it may turn out to be something else entirely. We can acknowledge that all Christians are called to ministry. And we can affirm that at this moment, the young person feels led in a certain direction and is making a certain commitment. We can work with our denominational leaders in providing resources for those who feel called to the ministry. We can also steer the young person to special events designed to help young people make sense of their calls.

## *Mission and Service*

Anyone who has been on a mission trip or in a mission experience with young people knows the potential of these experiences for spiritual growth. In spiritual autobiographies, mission trips rank high as moments of feeling close to God. Many of us have experienced testimonies of youth who say that the most powerful spiritual growth experiences in their lives have been connected to mission trip and service activities.

Involving young people in mission experiences can bring them closer to God. They can see Christ in their neighbor. God is not just experienced through the Bible, prayer, and worship. God is very much at work in the world, and involving young people in mission work can help bring the God of the Scriptures to life.

To ensure that the mission experience leads to spiritual growth, it is vital that there be opportunities to talk about and reflect upon the experience in light of the Christian faith. Seeing any mission experience as an opportunity for spiritual growth, and taking the time to debrief it, can greatly enhance the spirituality of the young people with whom we work.

## *Trips and Retreats*

Trips, camps, and retreats provide the "mountain-top experiences" of youth ministry. While our relationship with God cannot be limited to these experiences, they can play a crucial role in adolescent faith. If given the choice between having a young person in Sunday school for six months or having the same youth in a camp for a week, many of us would choose the camp experience. The camp experience is that powerful and life transforming.

As youth workers, we find it important to both encourage our youth to participate in these experiences and provide the opportunity to debrief the experiences. Most church denominations and other Christian groups provide high-quality spiritual growth experiences at camps and retreats. Making sure that our youth are involved in these experiences adds a dimension that we alone cannot provide. However, debriefing these experiences is crucial. The youth have the emotional experience. But we need to help them make sense of the experience and translate what it means in terms of their life back at home, at school, and at church.

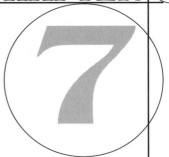

# CHAPTER

# A SPIRITUAL LIFE RETREAT

Early in my ministry I had the privilege of going through a nine-month, spiritual-formation program sponsored by Perkins School of Theology in Dallas, Texas. That program introduced me to the historic spiritual disciplines of our faith and to many of the contemporary developments in Christian spirituality.

Near the end of that year, I was part of a design team for an area-wide spiritual life retreat for youth. This opportunity allowed me to incorporate many of the ideas and techniques gleaned from the course (and included in this book) and apply them to a weekend retreat for junior and senior high youth.

This retreat model has been widely used by a number of people in a variety of situations. It is included here as a model that incorporates many of the ideas suggested in this book and one that can be readily adapted to a variety of settings. The retreat was built around the following elements:

- Small groups for sharing
- Journaling
- A variety of prayer techniques
- Bible study
- Fasting
- Meditation
- Worship
- Spiritual growth gathering

The following material, containing the daily schedule and a detailed description of the retreat activities, is the leader's guide for the retreat. Provide each youth a Bible, a pen or pencil, a simple inexpensive notebook or several sheets of paper, and copies of the materials on pages 124–129. Use the retreat as written, or draw from this outline ideas to help you design and lead your own spiritual life retreat with youth.

## *Retreat Schedule*

**Friday**

| | |
|---|---|
| 7:00 p.m. | Registration |
| 8:00 p.m. | Orientation |
| 8:15 p.m. | Group-building activities |
| 8:45 p.m. | Community experience |
| 9:00 p.m. | Spiritual family session |
| 10:45 p.m. | Break |
| 11:30 p.m. | Worship |
| Midnight | In rooms |
| 12:30 a.m. | Bed check and lights out |

**Saturday**

| | |
|---|---|
| 8:00 a.m. | Breakfast |
| 8:45 a.m. | Worship |
| 9:15 a.m. | Solitude |
| 10:00 a.m. | Community experience |
| 10:30 a.m. | Spiritual family session |
| 12:30 p.m. | Lunch |
| 1:00 p.m. | Recreation |
| 3:00 p.m. | Worship |
| 3:30 p.m. | Solitude |
| 4:30 p.m. | Free time |
| 6:00 p.m. | Supper |
| 6:30 p.m. | Community experience |
| 7:00 p.m. | Spiritual family session |
| 9:00 p.m. | Fellowship Time |
| 10:30 p.m. | In rooms |
| 11:30 p.m. | Bed check and lights out |

**Sunday**

| | |
|---|---|
| 8:00 a.m. | Breakfast |
| 9:00 a.m. | Solitude |
| 9:30 a.m. | Community experience |
| 10:00 a.m. | Spiritual family session |
| 11:00 p.m. | Solitude |
| 11:30a.m. | Closing worship |

# *Friday Evening*
## Is Something Missing?

### Registration (1 hour)
Assign rooms; distribute pencils and student notebooks. Organize activities such as volleyball, Frisbee®, hikes, and so on, if you choose.

### Orientation (15 minutes)
Welcome all of the students to the retreat. Briefly review the rules, schedule, and student notebooks.

### Group-Building Activities (30 minutes)
Offer a time for fun and getting acquainted. Sing lively, high-energy songs. Then involve the members in group-building activities that enable them to get to know one another. It is especially helpful if you can get them into the small groups that they will be in for the weekend.

An example of a crowd breaker: Divide the participants into small groups of six to eight students. Ask the small groups to form circles. Have each person tell:

- His or her name
- One bit of personal information that no one else knows
- Something he or she has found that has helped him or her feel closer to God in the past
- A word or image that describes each person's relationship with God right now
- Why he or she came this weekend and what he or she hopes to receive

Go around the circle once for each of the questions. This will give the group members time to think about their answers and keep the sharing moving without focusing too much or too little on anyone.

In this manner, you begin at a comfortable, non-threatening pace, and then move toward talking openly and more deeply about their relationships with God. This kind of sharing may be new and difficult for some of your group members.

You're trying to set the tone for your group for the rest of the sessions; so keep the group moving toward sharing, without pushing too hard.

## *Community Experience (15 minutes)*

### Guided Fantasy
Ask for volunteers to read aloud John 1:1-5; 8:14, 16-18. Explain that you will be taking them on a guided fantasy, based on these verses. Ask them to relax, close their eyes, listen, and imagine, as you guide them. Slowly say the following:

God is the creator and source of all that is. God is *your* creator. God gave you the gift of life. Experience the preciousness and sacredness of that gift. . . .

God has been present all your life. In some ways, you have known that and responded. Think of a time when you felt close to God. . . . Feel God's joy and love at that moment. . . .

In many ways, we have missed that presence. We've not known God, not accepted God. Think of a time when you felt cut off from God, distant and alone. Feel God's sadness at the moment. . . .

God is here with you now—in the world, in your life. You can come to know God—experience God's presence in a way you never dreamed possible. . . .

God offers you grace—power to become what God desires for you. Imagine what your relationship with God could be. . . . What is God's wish for you? How do you feel? . . .

## *Spiritual Family Session (1¾ hours)*

### Writing Spiritual Autobiographies

To move toward a deeper level, have the group members take ten to fifteen minutes to write a spiritual autobiography—a history of their relationship with God.

Ask the students to open their notebooks and use "My Spiritual Autobiography" (see page 124) as their guide for reflecting and writing. Explain that they are to focus on their faith journey—their relationship with God as best as they are aware of it— and what has helped or hindered that relationship.

The autobiographies don't have to be in complete sentences. The students are to strive for insights and notes on each of the eight areas on the worksheet. In addition, they are to think of anything else that has had an effect on their spiritual journey. The object of this assignment is to give them material to talk about. Call time at the end of fifteen minutes even if the youth are not finished. It is important to have plenty of time for discussion. Persons can fill in verbally what they did not have time to write.

### Talking About Spiritual Autobiographies

Ask each person to tell about his or her spiritual autobiography. Facilitate the discussion by going first then asking for volunteers. After each person has talked, open the group for questions and comments. Be alert for times when one member's story touches the other members' stories. Continue until everyone has had an opportunity to tell about his or her autobiography. Watch the clock. Be sure to proportion the time so that everyone in the group has the same opportunity to tell about his or her journey.

After hearing all of the stories, initiate a discussion on insights or comment on the autobiographies as a whole. If you have a group that speaks easily, use time in the second session to finish this exercise, if need be.

## Introducing the Idea of Spiritual Growth

In this exercise, you'll begin teaching about spiritual growth and introduce the concept of spiritual disciplines. Present the following in your own words. Say something like:

> Spiritual growth or formation is based on the idea that you can become closer to God than you now are.
>
> For centuries, Christians have used specific tools to develop and grow in their relationship with God. These are called spiritual disciplines, means of grace, or practices of the faith. These spiritual disciplines can be paralleled with other disciplines that you are familiar with—athletics, music, or study. You know from your own experience that in any area of life in which you want to grow and become stronger, you need to practice. That takes discipline.
>
> The ideas of spiritual growth, formation, and spiritual disciplines may be new to some of you, but you are already familiar with many of the disciplines. We have just used two: guided imagery using Scripture and group sharing.
>
> How many other spiritual disciplines can you name? What are some of the things Christians practice, things we do regularly? *(Prayer, meditation, fasting, Bible study, confession, worship, journaling, solitude, service, guidance)*
>
> We will be using and experiencing many of these this weekend. Are there any questions?"

## First Prayer Journal Assignment

Introduce the idea of a prayer journal: a diary of one's relationship with God and one's spiritual life. Underscore the importance of solitude—a time to be alone with God, away from all distractions. Explain that during the periods of solitude, the participants can focus their attention on God through the use of prayer journals.

Explain that during the journaling time, they will be able to think about their relationship with God; pray to God (on paper); and, most important, begin to listen to God.

Say that the journal assignments will be an important part of the weekend. Inform them that the results of the exercises will be discussed in the small group sessions.

Ask the students to turn to their copy of "Prayer Journal—Assignment 1" (pages 125–126). Read aloud the definition of a prayer journal, as it is written on the page. Go over the instructions for the assignments. Tell the youth that they will have solitude and time to work on the prayer journal in the morning. Be clear about having them bring their Bibles, notebooks, instructions, and pencils with them to worship time.

## Closing Prayer for the Session

Ask the group members to stand in a circle with their arms around one another. Beginning with the person on your right, ask each person to say a prayer remembering the needs, pains, and joys heard from the person on his or her right, during the session. Go around the circle and ask each youth to participate.

Close the prayer yourself. Then lead the group in the prayer of Saint Francis by lining it out—you say each line, and the group repeats after you.

## The Prayer of St. Francis

Lord,
>   make me an instrument of thy peace;
>   where there is hatred, let me sow love;
>   where there is injury, pardon;
>   where there is doubt, faith;
>   where there is despair, hope;
>   where there is darkness, light;
>   where there is sadness, joy.

O Divine Master,
>   grant that I may not so much seek
>   to be consoled as to console;
>   to be understood, as to understand;
>   to be loved, as to love;
>   for it is in giving that we receive,
>   it is in pardoning that we are pardoned,
>   and it is in dying that we are born to eternal life.

End with a group hug, followed by individual hugs.

## Break (45 minutes)

## Worship (30 minutes)

Open with several praise songs. Build the worship around the Scriptures used during the last session and the theme, "Is Something Missing?" Ask one or two students to talk about their spiritual autobiographies and what they learned from the experience. Allow one or two others to talk about insights from the guided fantasy. Close with a song and prayer..

*"On spiritual life retreats, you get to leave the real world. Only those who are really involved in the church go, and there are fewer distractions during services. Retreats are a place where you can start new friendships and renew old ones. You can be yourself. Without your real world disguise, you are open to God's love and his plan for you."*

*Keithen, age 16*

# *Saturday Daytime*
## Listening to God Through the Bible

## Breakfast (45 minutes)

## Worship (30 minutes)
Open with several songs. Explore the idea of solitude: being alone, listening to God. Tell the students that they will have an opportunity for forty-five minutes of solitude after the worship. Say that they can work on their prayer journal assignment or just listen and relax. Close with the song "Humble Yourself" or another song that speaks of humility or solitude or listening to God.

## Solitude (45 minutes)
Ask the retreat members to go off for a time alone to watch nature, pray, read Scripture, and spend some quiet time alone. The materials they are to use are found in "Prayer Journal—Assignment 1."

## *Community Experience (30 minutes)*

## Singing
Use a song or two to bring the group back together. When everyone returns from their solitude time, take them through the following experiences:

## Relaxation Exercises
Use exercises such as toe touches, stretches, and deep breathing.

## Guided Fantasy
Lead the youth on a guided fantasy based on John 3:1-21. Retell the Nicodemus story. Ask the youth to imagine that they are Nicodemus. Slowly read the following:

"I am Nicodemus; I seek Jesus out by night. Why am I seeking Jesus? What questions do I have of him? What am I looking for? Why come by night? Who do I not want to see me? Am I ashamed? embarrassed? . . .

"I meet Jesus. What does he look like? Does he welcome me? What do I feel in his presence? . . .

"Jesus makes a puzzling statement, " Unless you change, you cannot enter my kingdom." Born again? How? That's impossible! Why does he say this to me? What is he really trying to say? What do I need to change in my life? How should I be different? . . .

"Jesus talks about two kinds of life. What in my life is worldly? What in my life is spiritual? How can I believe in what I've not seen? . . .

"God loves me so much, he sent his son. For me? What is Jesus offering me? What am I missing? What is God telling me? How can Jesus make a difference in my life?"

## *Spiritual Family Session (2 hours)*

### Reactions

Discuss the guided fantasy. The group has just come out of an experience that was new for many of them. Begin your spiritual family session by inviting the youth to talk about their experience, feelings, insights, and reactions to the fantasy.

Ask:

- What was it like? Weird? Nice? Explain.
- How does this experience compare with the way we usually use the Bible. What's the difference? Which do they prefer?
- Do you usually read the Bible with the expectation that God will actually "speak" to you? Is that a new idea for any of you?
- What do you think about reading the Bible in this way?

Explain that a guided fantasy is one form of a devotional Bible study—reading the Bible in such a way that you expect God to speak to you personally through the story.

Tell your group members that they are going to experience another guided fantasy, one in which Jesus would offer them something that could change their lives.

### Guided Fantasy

Ask three young people to read aloud John 4:1-26; 6:26-27, 34-35. Invite the group members to get comfortable, either in their chairs or on the floor.

Slowly read aloud the following meditation. Feel free to change or adapt it as you wish. Use the ellipses (. . .) for pauses to let your group members' imaginations go to work.

"Feel yourself falling, . . . falling back through time, . . . farther . . . to a far distant land long ago. . . . You're thirsty. . . . You go over to a water bucket for a drink, but it's empty. . . . You decide to go down to the well outside of town to get some water and bring it back. . . . You leave your home, . . . step out into the street, . . . feel the heat, . . . hear the sounds of animals. . . . Which animals can you hear? . . . Can you see them? . . . You can smell someone cooking lunch. . . . What are they cooking? . . . What is someone arguing about? . . . You're now outside of town, headed for the well. . . . You hear birds singing. . . . It's so hot. . . . You're thirsty. . . . You look up, and there is someone sitting at the well, . . . a stranger. He looks tired and thirsty. . . . He's Jewish! . . . Your people and his people have hated one another for centuries. . . . Feel the anger inside. . . . Is he dangerous? . . . Do you feel fear? . . . He doesn't look dangerous. . . . You know that he hates you. . . . All Jews hate your people; they always have. . . . He's saying something to you. . . . He wants you to get him a bucket of water. . . . You have a bucket and he doesn't. . . . 'What? You, a Jew, ask me, a Samaritan, for a drink?' . . . Before you realize it, those words have slipped out. . . . Strange, he doesn't seem mad. He's smiling. . . . Now he's speaking to you again. . . . 'If you only knew what God is offering you right now, you'd be asking me for a drink, . . . a drink of what I can offer you, . . . a drink of living water. . . . You find yourself wondering, 'What's water got to do with God?' . . . God is offering me something right now? . . . What is living water? . . . And who is this guy, talking about living water and doesn't even have his own bucket? . . . He's speaking again. . . . 'Whoever drinks from this well will get thirsty again, but anyone who drinks what I have to give will never be thirsty again. . . . What I have to give is eternal life.' . . . What kind of water is that, . . . to never be thirsty again, . . . to never feel empty (and at times I feel so empty), . . . to be satisfied, . . . at peace. . . . You hear yourself asking for some of this special water. . . . He starts speaking to you again. . . . You can't believe what you're hearing! . . . He knows! . . . Your deepest, darkest secret, . . . he knows! . . . How? . . . How does he know that? . . . Who is this man? . . . Is he some kind of prophet? . . . He's speaking to you again. . . . 'You worship God one way, and I worship God another. . . . I worship the God I know; you worship a God you've never really known, . . . never really experienced, . . . never really loved.' . . . How does he know these things about me? . . . He's still speaking. . . . 'The time will come, in fact, is here now, when you will no longer worship God the way you have in the past. . . . No, from now on, you will worship God in spirit and in truth.' . . . You find yourself praying, 'Oh, God, I wish it were true. . . . Can I really feel close to you? . . . Can I be close to you?' Who is this man? 'Your Christ will come. . . . We all look forward to that day when we can really know God and feel close to God.' . . . He speaks to you again, . . . 'I, who am speaking to you, whoever comes to me will never be hungry. Whoever believes in me will never thirst.' . . . You look into his eyes. . . . You know the hunger in your life, . . . the emptiness. . . . You know what you thirst for, . . . and he is offering it to you . . . right now" (long pause).

"Take a moment to bring yourself back into this gathering. When you are ready, come back to our group circle."

## Debriefing

Initiate a group discussion on the experience. Focus on some of the following questions:

- How did the use of the five senses at the beginning help you get into the story, make it more real?
- What was it like to place yourself in the story?
- What was it like to meet Jesus?
- Could you clearly identify your deepest, darkest secret? What is it like to think that Jesus knows even that about you?
- What does "living water" mean to you?
- What do you think God is offering now, here this weekend? Are you beginning to get an idea of what you can get in your relationship with God that you didn't have?

## Prayer Journal Discussion

Ask the youth if they understand the meaning and use of a prayer journal. Did the descriptions they were given in the first session help? What do they think about the idea of a prayer journal? Have any of the group members journaled in the past? If so, have them explain.

Were the group members able to write a letter to God? Was it difficult to do this? Have them explain. Ask if any of them will tell about his or her letter. Break the ice by telling about your own letter.

Probe to find how the group felt about moving beyond writing a letter to God to actually entering into a conversation with God. What was this like? What is it like to think of God speaking to you? Does it feel awkward to listen to God?

Would any of the group members be willing to tell about his or her conversation? You can facilitate this by going first in talking about your dialogue.

## Second Prayer Journal Assignment

Give directions for the second assignment for the prayer journal (page 127). Ask if there are any questions.

## Closing Prayer for the Session

Have everyone stand in a circle. Ask for favorite songs, then have the group sing one or two of them. Go around the circle in prayer, with each member lifting up concerns or sorrows that other members mentioned during the session. Close the prayer yourself. End with a group hug and individual hugs.


## Lunch (30 minutes)

## Recreation (2 hours)

This is an intense weekend for many youth. Use the time after lunch as a recreational time so that the retreat participants can unwind and drain off pent-up energy.

## Worship (30 minutes)

Open with a song. Build the service on the Scripture used in the session and the theme "Listening to God Through Devotional Bible Study." Allow a few participants to express their reactions to the guided fantasy and the first prayer journal assignment. Close with a song.

## Solitude (1 hour)

Ask group members to complete "Prayer Journal—Assignment 2."

## Free Time (1½ hours)

## Supper (30 minutes)

# Saturday Evening
## Listening to God Through Prayer

## Community Experience (30 minutes)

### Singing

Sing songs, moving to ones that are prayerful, such as "Sanctuary," to set the tone.

### Breathing Exercise

Lead the group in slow, deep breathing. Have the group try "breath Scripture" such as this from Psalm 46:10:

"Be still (inhale) and know (exhale) that I (inhale) am God (exhale)."

### Traditional Forms of Prayer

Introduce the following traditional forms of prayer and allow time for the students to imagine according to the directions:

**Praise and Thanksgiving:** Feel God's love, God's joy. . . . Give thanks to God for. . . .

**Confession and Pardon:** Measure your life by what God would like you to be. . . . Where are disappointments? Feel God's sadness. . . . Lift these to the Lord. . . . Receive God's forgiveness. . . . Feel God s forgiveness enter you. . . . Imagine God hugging you. . . . Imagine love flowing through your veins. . . .

**Petition:** Ask for God's help in some area of your life. . . . Imagine God's love embracing you without words. . . . Feel God's strength and power flowing into you. . . . Feel your problem growing smaller as God's power grows stronger. . . .

**Intercession:** Think of someone in your group or at home who has a problem. Ask God's help for that person. . . . Image God's love embracing him or her. . . . Imagine God's power and strength flowing into that person. . . . Imagine his or her problem or pain growing weaker as the power of God grows. . . .

### New Ways to Pray

Introduce these ways to pray. Allow time for the students to imagine and practice.

**Centering Prayer:** Focus on the center of your body. . . . Release tension; be at peace. . . . Feel peace flow out from your center. . . .

**Emptying Prayer:** Relax; release tension. . . . Remove everything from awareness. . . . Be empty, silent. . . . Dwell in empty silence. . . . Listen to silence. . . . Listen to God. . . .

**Jesus Prayer:** "Lord Jesus, have mercy upon me, a sinner." . . . Repeat this over and over in your mind. . . . See if any word stands out, if any images or thoughts come. . . . Let your imagination go. . . . Go with whatever comes into your mind. . . .

**Mantra:** Lift up one word in your mind, such as *life, love, peace, joy.* . . . Repeat the word over and over in your mind. . . . Begin to feel what the word means. . . . Feel life, love, peace, joy. . . . Dwell in the feeling. . . . Let it flow over you into you, . . . through you. . . .

## *Spiritual Family Session (2 hours)*

### Debriefing

Begin the session by asking the group members to tell their experiences and reactions to the prayer exercises. Incorporate the following questions:

- Which of the exercises were new to you?
- Which did you find difficult to get into?
- Which did you not enjoy?
- Which did you enjoy or find particularly helpful? Explain.
- Which was the most vivid or powerful?
- How does this way of praying compare with the way you usually pray?
- What do you think about this approach?
- Which of these could you use in your own prayer life?
- What are your reactions, thoughts, or feelings about prayer as listening to God, rather than telling God something.

### The Importance of Listening

Ask the group to discuss what it takes to make a good friend. What do they look for in a good friendship? What does it take to maintain a good friendship?

Once the group has a good idea of what friendship is and what it needs, ask what the group thinks about the following three qualities in a friendship:

- Time together
- "Quality time" (away from all distractions)
- Listening

Ask the group members to think about their relationship with God as an intimate friendship. Ask what they can lift up from the discussion on friendship and apply to their relationship with God. Do we nurture our friendship with God? Do we take time with God? Do we have "quality time" away from all distractions? Do we ever listen to God, really expecting that God can speak to us? What kind of clutter do we allow to get in the way of our friendship with God?

## Prayer Journal Discussion

Have the group members tell about their journaling experiences. Were they able to use the devotional Bible study techniques to make the Scripture more real? What happened when they placed themselves in the story? What gets in the way of their friendship with God? Could they identify anything they feel might offend Jesus?

## Cleansing the Temple

Explain that one of the primary goals of the spiritual disciplines is to create a place in our lives where God can speak to us, to remove all the clutter—all the conflicting claims on our time and our energy so that we make room and time to be with God.

Four of the spiritual disciplines are specifically intended to remove the noises and distractions that keep us from listening to God. As you go over these four disciplines below, the idea is to find if any of these could be useful in getting rid of some of the distracting clutter that we have identified. (The goals are to initate discussion now and to open new possibilities for the youth for spiritual growth in the long term.)

**Solitude:** Give the group the following definition of *solitude*:

> *Solitude,* as a spiritual discipline, means to spend time alone, in silence, listening to God. It is a deliberate stepping back from all of the activities, people, distractions, and noise of our normal day so that we can spend some quality time with God.

Your group has now had two opportunities for solitude this weekend. Ask the group members to tell what those experiences were like. Ask if any of them experiences solitude at home—being completely alone, in silence (no stereo, radio, or television). What's that experience like at home? Could the experience be negative (lonely)? What regular times of solitude would add to their relationship with God that is not already there? What clutter might it remove?

**Fasting:** Ask the group what *fasting* means. Then give the following definition:

> *Fasting,* a spiritual discipline, means to abstain from food for a set period of time for spiritual purposes—not to lose weight or to make a political point (as in a hunger strike). The spiritual purpose of fasting is to heighten awareness of God's presence and free us from a preoccupation with food.

To better understand how fasting can heighten awareness, ask if they have ever eaten so much that they became sleepy or sluggish. Explain that not eating, especially for a long period of time, can do the opposite—it can make a person more alert and aware.

**119**

Ask if any of the group members has ever fasted. If so, ask him or her to talk about the experience. Encourage the group to ask questions of those who have fasted. If no one in the group has fasted, you might reveal some of the following information:

Those who do fast say that it can make us more alert and aware of things around us and with us, including God's presence. People who fast find that after twenty-four to forty-eight hours of fasting, it is much easier to pray. Fasting also can free us from a preoccupation with food. Most of us spend a good amount of our time eating, talking about food, preparing food, or thinking about food, which consumes a lot of our time and energy. Many people are surprised to discover that they don't need to eat three times a day. After a day or so, the person who is fasting may not even be hungry and may find that his or her energy level has increased.

Initiate a discussion on fasting. What are fears and myths about fasting? Is it a spiritual discipline the youth might like to try?

**Simplicity:** Read the following quotation from *Celebration of Discipline: Paths to Spiritual Growth, 20th Anniversary Edition,* by Richard J. Foster (Harper San Francisco, 1988; ISBN 0060628391):

> Simplicity is freedom. . . . Because we lack a divine Center our need for security has led us into an insane attachment to things. We really must clearly understand that the lust for affluence in contemporary society is psychotic. It is psychotic because it has completely lost touch with reality. We crave things we neither need nor enjoy. "We buy things we do not want to impress people we do not like." . . . We are made to feel ashamed to wear clothes or drive cars until they are worn out. The mass media have convinced us that to be out of step with fashion is to be out of step with reality.

Ask whether Foster is overstating the case. Is happiness to be found in more and more "things"? If we have enough, own enough, possess enough, if there is enough money in our bank account, will we be happy? How much is "enough"? Get the group to think about these questions for a few minutes.

As a spiritual discipline, simplicity affirms that more "things" cannot make us happy; in fact, possessions can clutter up our lives and lead us away from what's really important. In our society, many believe that the importance or worth of a person is measured by the wealth or the amount of possessions. The discipline of simplicity says that this measure is not true.

Ask if the group can identify ways in which the "lust for affluence" makes relationships with other people and with God more difficult. Do they experience this in their school? churches? families? Where else?

How could this discipline help their personal relationship with God? What clutter could it remove from their lives?

**Submission:** Read the following definition of *submission*:

> Another word for *submission* is *servanthood*. As a spiritual discipline, submission affirms that the way to self-fulfillment is through self-denial—to hold others' interests above one's self-interest.

Initiate a discussion on this definition. Is the idea offensive? naive? After everyone has had an opportunity to react, ask if any of them has ever encountered a person who seemed completely absorbed with himself or herself. Have the group members talk about their experiences.

Have the youth ever known someone who seemed to value them as much as the person values himself or herself? If they have, have them describe how they knew they were valued and how being honored like that felt. If not, have them fantasize what it might he like to know such a person.

Encourage the youth to consider the idea of a group—like your group—in which all of the members are more concerned about one another than about themselves.How could the discipline of submission help their relationship with God? What clutter could it help remove?

## Third Prayer Journal Assignment

Ask the students to turn to their copy of the third prayer journal assignment (page 128). Ask if there are any questions.

## Closing Prayer for the Session

Have everyone stand in a prayer circle. Sing a song such as "We Are the Family of God." Go around the circle in a prayer, having each member lift the concerns they heard during the session. Close the prayer yourself. End with hugs.

## Fellowship Time (1½ hours)

Allow some open fellowship time during the evening. This could include an afterglow setting, with snacks and a time just to visit and have fellowship. You might include informal singing or any other activity that you feel would be appropriate to the event.

# *Sunday Morning*
## Listening to God Within "the Body"

## Breakfast, Pack, Load (1 hour)

## Solitude (30 minutes)

Ask group members to complete "Prayer Journal—Assignment 3."

# *Community Experience*

## Relaxation and Guided Fantasy

Ask the group members to lie on the floor so that each one is both supporting and supported by others. Slowly read aloud John 15:1-8. Take them on a guided fantasy:

"Imagine yourself as the branch. You are drawing nourishment and strength from God (the vine). . . . Feel the strength flowing in, . . . flowing into your feet, . . . up through your body, . . . out of your arms and head, . . . flowing into you, through you to others around you. . . . You're being supported by other branches around you, . . . by the bodies you are lying on. . . . You are not alone. . . . You are surrounded, supported. . . . Feel that support. . . . Feel strength, nourishment flowing into you from those around you. . . . Feel the connection between you and everyone else here, . . . all a part of the vine, . . . God's strength flowing into you from others, . . . flowing to others from you. . . . "

Ask the youth to keep their eyes closed as you read 1 Corinthians 12:12-30. Then take them on a second guided fantasy:

"Imagine yourself as one small part of a body. . . . Feel the other parts of the body around you, . . . so small, dependent on the other parts for nourishment, . . . for help, . . . for life. . . . You can't say to others, 'I don't need you.' . . . Cut off from others, you would die, . . . so small, yet important. . . . You have your part to do. . . . Without you, the work would not get done. . . . Feel the others who rest on you depend on you for support. . . . No one can say to you, 'I don't need you.' . . . Without you, the body would not be whole. . . . Feel a sense of belonging. . . . You are a part of the body. . . . Feel your place, how you are connected to all around you. . . ."

## *Spiritual Family Session (1 hour)*

### Debriefing
Ask the group to debrief the two guided fantasies:

**The Vine:**
- What was it like to be a part of the vine? Could you feel the strength flowing into you? Does that ever really happen to you? Explain.
- What was it like to feel yourself supported by others? Where do you get that in real life? at home? in school? at church? in youth group? Here?
- Have you ever felt cut off from the vine and other branches? What was that like?
- How important is being a part of the vine to you personally? Could you be more attached than you are? more supported?

**The Body:**
- Compare "the body" exercise with "the vine" exercise. How were they different? similar?
- What's it like to have to depend on others?
- What's it like to have others depend on you?
- Are you needed? important? Do you have a contribution to make?

## Prayer Journal Discussion

Ask the group members to tell how God has come to them in other people in the past. Guide the discussion with the following questions. You will use these questions to set up the next exercise.

- What did these people do?
- How are these people different from others?
- Do you think that God has ever used you in someone else's life?
- Has God worked through any of you this weekend?

## Spiritual Healing Exercise

Ask the group members to sit in a circle on the floor. Ask for a volunteer. The volunteer is to tell one hurt or need that he or she has. The rest of the group is to try to listen and understand that hurt. The youth cannot give advice or try to solve the problem. They can ask questions to try to understand the problem better, and they can tell their concerns. When the person feels that the group has heard and understands his or her problem, he or she should lie down or kneel in the middle of the circle while everyone else places one hand on him or her. Each person in the group then gives a verbal prayer for the person in the center. The prayer lifts up the pain or problem and asks for healing. When the prayer is finished, have the person in the center express what the experience was like for him or her. Repeat the process with other volunteers.

## Fourth Prayer Journal Assignment

Ask the students to turn to their copy of the fourth prayer journal assignment (page 129). Ask if there are any questions.

## Closing Prayer for the Session

Have the group get into a circle and begin with a song such as "Lord, I Lift Your Name on High."

Join in a prayer circle, giving thanks for the weekend. Close the prayer yourself, and lead the group in the Lord's Prayer. Close with a group hug and individual hugs.

## Solitude (30 minutes)

Give the group time to complete the fourth prayer journal assignment before they go to worship.

## Closing Worship for the Retreat (30 minutes).

Open with a song. Build the service on any Scriptures used this weekend and the theme "Spiritual Growth—Reaching Out." Allow time for the students to reach out to the two people they identified in their fourth prayer journal assignment. Close with several of the songs that were sung during the retreat.

# My Spiritual Autobiography

Follow the nine steps below to trace your spiritual journey—the history of your relationship with God. You have only a few minutes, so don't worry about writing complete sentences. Just get enough down on paper so that you can talk about your faith journey with the other members of your group. Feel free to use anything that came to mind during the guided fantasy. Write down anything that you think is relevant, but be sure to include the following items:

1. My earliest memory or awareness of God
2. The major religious events or experiences in my life (family, church, youth group, camp, and so on)
3. My spiritual high point (time when I felt closest to God)
4. My spiritual low point (time when I felt most distant from God)
5. Special people who have played a role in my faith journey
6. Where I am right now in my relationship with God
7. Where I would like to be in my relationship with God
8. What's missing in my relationship with God
9. Struggles I have in my faith or my walk with God

# Prayer Journal—Assignment 1

**1. What is a "prayer journal"?** Read the following descriptions:

*A journal is a personal record of feelings, thoughts, concerns, and visions, often written as a letter to God. Journal writing is a way of capturing the inner person to gain self-understanding. It includes any and every part of life but is more concerned with meaning than with events, especially ultimate meaning.*

*All writing is just talking put on paper. Many times, we are not sure what we think until we say it. A journal is a safe place to face the parts of ourselves that we don't talk about anywhere else.*

*Writing in a journal or keeping a journal is a method that facilitates my taking time and effort to be honest with myself before God.*

*Writing in my journal is a prayer form for me. Prayer becomes attention to presence—not only God's but your own. . . . The transcendent, which we so often neglect and for which we have such deep yearning, is not only where God lives, but where we live when we are most alive.*

What in those statements stands out and speaks to you personally? Why? Write your responses on the back side of this sheet or on another sheet of paper.

If anything is unclear, make a note so that you can bring it up in your next spiritual family session.

**2. Write a letter to God.** Review your spiritual autobiography. Focus on the parts in which you talked about where you are now in your relationship with God, where you would like to be, and what's missing in that relationship. Add what you hope you can get here this weekend in the way of spiritual enrichment. Talk to God about what you discovered as you did your autobiography and reviewed the questions. Talk to God as you would to any close friend.

Dear God,

**3. Have a conversation with Jesus.** Read the following conversation with Jesus:

**Me:** Where's the burning bush when I need it? I want signs, like the people in the Bible got.

**Jesus:** I can see you are upset. What, exactly, is bothering you? Tell me about it.

**Me:** I don't know what to do. I need someone to tell me. But then I really don't want someone to tell me. I guess I just want to feel sure that the decisions I make are the right ones. Moses couldn't miss the message of the burning bush. It was clear what he needed to do. I wish I could know so clearly. I just feel all mixed up.

**Jesus:** You're OK. You don't have to he perfect. You don't have to know everything. Just know I love you. I love and accept you here, now, always. Listen to your heart. Let my love guide you. Make the best decision you can and trust in my grace to keep working for the best.

**Me:** Thank you, Jesus. I feel like you've just lifted a big weight off my shoulders. I don't feel so alone.

**Jesus:** Good, because you are not alone. I am with you—always.

Go back and reread your letter to God. Write a dialogue (like the one above) in which you share your biggest concern in the letter and have Jesus respond. If you experience difficulty having Jesus respond, take a few moments of silence and see if some reply comes—something that Jesus might say.

Me:

Jesus:

Me:

Jesus:

Me:

Jesus:

**4. Read John 3:1-21.** Read the passage and place yourself in the story. You become Nicodemus. You have the conversation with Jesus. What do you hear Jesus saying to you? Write a dialogue with Jesus, if you wish. When you have finished, close with a silent prayer.

# Prayer Journal—Assignment 2

**1. Take a few minutes to center yourself**—experience solitude, enjoy being alone. When you're ready, do the following exercise:

**2. Read John 2:13-16.** Read the passage over again, using each of your senses. If you had been there, what would you have seen? heard? smelled? tasted? Place yourself in the story. Where would you have been? Who would you have been? What would you have felt? done? Journal the results of your meditations.

Use the Temple as an image for your life. What is there that shouldn't be? What clutters up your life and keeps you from what's really important? What in your life do you think would really offend Jesus? Identify as many things as possible. Write them down.

**3. Journal a prayer to God.** Lift up the clutter you see that keeps you from having the kind of relationship with God that you would like to have.

Dear God,

**4. Concentrate.** Close your eyes, center yourself, and mentally go over what you've written. Use a period of silence to see if you can "hear" God speak to you about what bothers you. If that's difficult, try journaling a conversation with God about the clutter in your life.

Me:

Jesus:

Me:

Jesus:

Me:

Jesus:

**5. Offer a silent prayer.**

# Prayer Journal—Assignment 3

**1. Answer these questions:** How has God come to you through other people? How have people been important in your faith journey? Review your autobiography. Who has helped you? Name specific people, events, and experiences. What was it about these persons that made them instruments of God in your life? Were they special in any way? Journal what you uncover.

**2. Review the weekend.** Who has God used for you this weekend? How has God used them? Do you think that God has used you this weekend to help anyone else? Write your answers.

**3. Read 1 Corinthians 12:12-30.** How has God used "the body" (the church, your youth group, camp, individual Christians) in your life? How has God used you to help others?

**4. Write a prayer letter to God.** Lift up what you've discovered during this assignment.

Dear God,

**5. Close with a silent prayer.**

# Prayer Journal—Assignment 4

**1. Read John 21:15-17.**
Identify someone in your church or youth group who needs help and support; be very specific. What does the person need?

Identify someone at the retreat (who is not in your group) who needs help and support. Write how you can help meet this need before you leave today. Be aware that you will be given an opportunity to reach out to these people during the closing worship service.

**2. Review the weekend—all that you have learned and experienced.** In the space below, write what you will take home with you from this weekend to use in your spiritual journey. Note any commitments you've made.

# CHAPTER

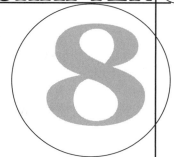

# SILVER BULLETS FOR SPIRITUAL GROWTH

A generation ago Karl Rohnke, with Project Adventure, published a book entitled *Silver Bullets,* which contained a variety of activities developed at ropes challenge courses. The book picked up on the old imagery from the werewolf mythology that stated that a werewolf could be killed only by a silver bullet. Rohnke's point was a valid one—that there are activities and exercises that are wonderful at accomplishing a specific task.

Over the past thirty-plus years in youth ministry, I have added to my personal bag of tricks several silver bullets for spiritual growth. These are zero-risk activities. They work time after time, across the years, and in a wide variety of settings. Many of these activities are available in other places. But they are often not thought of as tools for spiritual growth and formation. In addition, it may be helpful to have them gathered in one place.

The following is an overview; each of these silver bullets is given with more detail later in the chapter:

## Peter's Walk

Peter's Walk has been around for many years. First published as an article by Joye Perry in *Youth Teacher and Counselor* in Summer 1986, it recently appeared in *Destination Easter!* (Abingdon Press, 1998) in a version revised by Billy and Laura Echols-Richter and myself based on the adaptations we have made over the years.

We often use this activity on the opening night of a spiritual life retreat. By reflecting on the life of Peter in an experiential way, the students begin to reflect on their own discipleship. After this two-hour experience, we find that the youth have already moved spiritually to a point we would expect them to be by the end of the weekend. Beginning with Peter's Walk enhances the entire retreat.

Peter's Walk is labor intensive and requires quite a bit of setup. You may want to have a team to help set up. The activity, however, is well worth the effort.

## Romans and Christians With Catacomb Worship

Romans and Christians has also been around for a long time. Most recently, Romans and Christians was published in *The Catacomb Project: Hope for 2000 and Beyond* (Abingdon Press, 1999). When I first encountered it in the early 1970's, it was a glorified tag game in the Capture the Flag mode. Over the years the game has evolved. For many youth, this simulation game is the first time they have been confronted about their faith . Like Peter's Walk, Romans and Christians requires a lot of setup and is adult intensive. But it also has immense power and can provide life-altering experiences.

The Catacomb Worship service picks up the imagery of Romans and Christians and brings it into a worship setting. It is a wonderful ending to the simulation.

## Trust Village

Trust Village was also created for a retreat setting but is now widely used in other places. Faith is defined as trusting, believing, and committing. Of the three, trust is probably the most basic. This activity provides an experiential exploration of the issue of trust.

## Four *Go For It!* Games

I have also included four exercises from my book *Go For It! Games: 25 Faith-Building Adventures for Groups* (Abingdon Press, 1998) that have particular value for spiritual growth. The key is the time for debriefing and making the faith link.

### 1. Lifeline and Unseen Hands

Lifeline raises the questions of what we hang on to in our faith journeys as well as what is trustworthy. Unseen Hands goes a step further to help youth recognize the help of the Holy Spirit in guiding them.

### 2. Abraham's Journey

Abraham's Journey asks: How does God speak to us? How do we know that a voice we hear is God's? How do we know what God is saying? .

### 3. The Shepherd's Voice

The Shepherd's Voice also deals with spiritual discernment, asking how we distinguish the voice of God from other voices, including ones that may be harmful.

### 4. 3-D Minefield

3-D Minefield takes the issue of spiritual guidance one step further. Using an obstacle course, this activity asks how good are we at giving spiritual guidance and direction and how good are we at receiving spiritual guidance and direction?

# *Peter's Walk*

This devotional experience for youth is a trust walk that can be implemented where many rooms can be set up prior to the experience. Small groups are blindfolded and led from room to room. At each room, Peter tells an incident about his walk with Jesus. This event is most effective when rooms and hallways are dark.

You will need blindfolds for each person and an adult guide for each five to seven participants. Gather together activity facilitators, adult guides, singers, and other helpers prior to the event so that they understand their roles.

### On the day of the event

Tell adult guides: "Our activity facilitators will guide us through the entire process. Your role will be to guide your group from room to room and to do the symbolic actions the facilitators request of you. If you were not at the training, know that you will be told what to do at each station. We will begin after we gather the total group in our main meeting room."

After the group is gathered, the voice of "Peter" reads or paraphrases the following introductions:

"The next hour we spend together as a group will be an experience where all of your five senses will be used at one time or another. It is to be an experience of trust, because each of you will be blindfolded. You are requested not to cheat; just trust your guides. The guides will arrive after your blindfolds are in place. It is not important that you know who they are, but it is important that you trust them to lead you through this experience. I ask that you do not talk; just listen, . . . and feel, . . . and smell, . . . and taste, . . . and experience for the next hour some of the feelings and experiences that the disciple Peter might have had as he walked and trusted his life with Jesus."

Place blindfolds on the participants. Place the youth in lines of five, with their hands resting on the shoulders of the person in front of them. Adult guides will lead the line. When the participants are ready to begin their walk, the adult guide reads aloud Peter's introductions:

"You don't know me. We've never formally met. You have read about my life, part of it, that is. You've never read about me as a child growing up, but you've heard about my life from the point where I met Jesus for the first time. Sometimes when people read about my life in the Bible, they make it sound kind of boring and ordinary, but it wasn't at all. It was fascinating, exciting, frustrating, perplexing, and even scary. I had no idea when I met Jesus that my life would change so much (even my name). I had always been called Simon, but Jesus told me that I would be called Peter, the Rock. Jesus didn't change only me. He changed everyone he met in some way. I wish that you could have met and known him like I did. He was so special. I have so many memories to tell about. Come with me now, . . . back in time; . . . and relive with me some of my memories."

## Room 1
*You will need pieces of bread in baskets.*

Begin the walk to Room 1. After the arrival, have the youth sit on the floor.

Read: "One of the greatest things about being a disciple was having everyone regard you as one Jesus' disciples. It made me feel so important. We used to have mobs of people following us everywhere. Some people just wanted a glimpse of Jesus. Others wanted to touch him. Some even wanted to be healed. Take, for instance, one day when we were outside a town and people had come out to hear Jesus preach and teach them. He was even doing miracles that day. It was lunchtime; but no one, except for one little boy, had brought food. Jesus told us to feed the crowds with the little boy's five loaves and two fish. We all thought that he was joking. There were thousands of people to feed, but he was really serious. I couldn't believe my eyes. He blessed the food, and we started handing it out to everyone. There was always more in our baskets. We even had leftovers to collect. To this day, it is hard for me to believe that it happened. But I saw it. And I ate some of that bread and fish, too!"

Read aloud Mark 6:41-42:

[41] Taking the five loaves and the two fish, he looked up to heaven, and blessed and broke the loaves, and gave them to his disciples to set before the people; and he divided the two fish among them all. [42] And all ate and were filled.

Feed the youth pieces of bread from the baskets. Begin the walk to Room 2.

## Room 2
*You will need a water source, water hoses, large sheets of plastic, and towels.*

Have the youth remain standing. Guides, remove the participants' shoes and socks.

Read: "When we had finally finished eating (all five thousand of us), Jesus told us to get into the boat and head for Bethsaida. He said that he'd get everybody else started home. I kind of wondered, as we shoved off, how or when or where we were supposed to meet him. I figured that he had probably told John, so I settled back in the boat to relax. Most of us in the boat were exhausted after working in that crowd all day, but none of us could sleep. We were still discussing all the baskets full of leftovers.

"By sundown, we were almost halfway across the lake. A strong wind from the south seemed to appear out of nowhere and it wasn't long before we all realized that a storm was on the way. We were scared to death. We were afraid that we would capsize and drown. When the storm seemed to be at its worst, we saw someone or something walking out on the water. We figured that it must be a ghost.

"But then we recognized Jesus' voice talking to us from out on the lake. I couldn't believe it. First, he had fed all of those people and now this. What a day this was turning out to be. And before I realized it, I heard myself yelling back to Jesus, "Hey, if it's really you, let me walk on the water to you." Jesus yelled back "OK!" By this time, I realized what I had said. I really didn't want to go out there, but I couldn't chicken out now. (After all, everybody was watching me. I had my reputation to consider.) So I stepped out. It was the strangest sensation not to sink down into the water. The wind picked up again, and the boat was drifting farther and farther away from me; and I panicked. Just about the time my head went under, I felt a strong hand reach down and pick me up. . . . All night long, all I could think of was that I had walked on water with Jesus and that no one would ever believe me."

Note: Guide the groups to the starting edge of the plastic, then let go. Let them walk on the water unaided most of the way. Then have other adults reach out with their hands and guide them off the plastic. Have towels at the end of the line for them to wipe their feet on. Guides, replace shoes and socks.

Walk to Room 3.

## Room 3

*You will need rocks.*

Have the youth stand in a large circle.

Read: "In the beginning when I was one of Jesus' disciples, the time of the day that I liked the best was after supper sitting around the fire. Jesus would be with the crowds all day, but in the evenings there were just the thirteen of us. We talked about what had happened that day, and we told jokes, and had such good times, and once in a while Jesus would share stories with us. No matter what he said or how he said it, I always learned something new. I remember one night in particular. . . . Jesus had been kind of quiet and as he stared into the fire I could tell he had something on his mind. Finally, he broke into our conversation with one question: "Who do people say that I am?" That wasn't a particularly easy question to answer because it seemed like everyone we knew had a different opinion. But we shared with him as best we could. Finally, he asked, "Who do you say that I am?" All of us just sat there. How could he ask us such a question? What kind of answer did he want? Finally I blurted out, "You're the Christ, the Messiah, the Son of the living God." There! I had said it. I'd been thinking about it for a long time, but finally I had told him.

"I thought some of the other disciples might laugh, but nobody did. And then Jesus . . . well, he told me I was blessed and that I would be known as Peter, the Rock, and then he said something even more strange. He told me that he would build his church upon me. What did that mean? How would he build his church on me? What did he mean by calling me 'the Rock'?"

Give each youth a rock to hold in his or her hand. Begin the walk to Room 4.

## Room 4

*You will need chairs (arranged in a circle), bowls of warm water, and towels.*

Have the youth sit in chairs. Pour warm water into bowls.

Read: "It was almost time for the Passover Feast. I've always liked the Passover Feast and I was looking forward to spending it with Jesus. Jesus had sent John and me on to Jerusalem to begin preparations. He had told us where to go, who we would find, and what to do. I had seen so many miracles, but here was another mysterious happening and I still couldn't understand how he knew to tell us all of that. It was such a strange evening when Jesus and the rest of the disciples arrived. Judas seemed awfully fidgety and Jesus much more somber than usual. Jesus got up from the table, wrapped his cloak around his waist, and poured water into a basin. He turned with the basin of water and a towel in his hands to face us. I couldn't help but blurt out, "Lord, are you going to wash our feet?" This didn't make any sense! He had just ridden into Jerusalem a few days before on a donkey—just like the promised king! Everyone had been shouting, "Hosanna! Blessed is he who comes in the name of the Lord." How could the King of Israel, our Messiah, even think about doing a servant's duty! No! He mustn't be our servant. He is our Messiah—and king!
"But Jesus said he had to . . . that if I was to be a part of his kingdom, I had to let him do that. I remember him looking at me waiting for me to consent and I said, "Well, if you must wash my feet, please wash my head and hands as well." I felt so unworthy and unclean. But Jesus said that wasn't necessary. I watched him as he washed my feet, . . . his hands lovingly doing that lowly servant's task. Why? Why did he have to do that?"

Have the guides wash the feet of each participant and then gently dry them off with towels.

Read aloud John 13:36-38.
[36] Simon Peter said to him, "Lord, where are you going?" Jesus answered, "Where I am going, you cannot follow me now; but you will follow afterward." [37] Peter said to him, "Lord, why can I not follow you now? I will lay down my life for you." [38] Jesus answered, "Will you lay down your life for me? Very truly, I tell you, before the cock crows, you will have denied me three times."

Begin the walk to Room 5.

## Room 5

*You will need a large block of wood or a beam, a hammer, adults to sing "Were You There?"*

Read: "A cock never crows without my remembering that awful night when Jesus was arrested. I guess I have always bragged a little too much or thought I was capable of doing more than I could do, but when Jesus told me that night in the upper room that I would deny him three times, I just couldn't believe it. After all the things

I had seen, . . . after all he had taught me, . . . after all we had been through, . . . I could never deny him. (*Pause.*)

"But I did and I remember the cock crowing. Three times I had said I didn't know him. I wonder if Jesus told me that just so I would know that he knew how really weak I still was. I tried so hard to be perfect, to be strong, to be the best disciple that Jesus would ever work with; but Jesus knew how stupid I felt sometimes. He knew how scared I was too. And maybe his telling me that it would happen was his way of saying that he understood. He would forgive me, and he would want me to keep working for him. The worst part of denying Jesus was never getting the chance to tell him how sorry I was, because they crucified him."

(*Drag a heavy board or beam, then drop it with a loud bang. Do three sets of heavy blows with the hammer—one for each hand and one for the feet.*)

Sing "Were You There?" (*Sing a cappella.*)

"It was all over now. All my dreams of the great Kingdom, all my popularity was gone because Jesus was dead. I had spent three years of my life with him, and I ended it by failing him. He was gone. Our future together was gone."

Say: "Return to the room where we will have our catacomb worship."

## Room 6

But that's not the end of the story. After Jesus' resurrection, we read these words from the Gospel of John (21:14-17):
(*Several extremely bright lights come on, bathing the group in intense light.*)

"This was now the third time that Jesus appeared to the disciples after he was raised from the dead.
When they had finished breakfast, Jesus said to Simon Peter, 'Simon son of John, do you love me more than these?' He said to him, 'Yes, Lord; you know that I love you.' Jesus said to him, 'Feed my lambs.' A second time he said to him, 'Simon son of John, do you love me?' He said to him, 'Yes, Lord; you know that I love you.' Jesus said to him, 'Tend my sheep.' He said to him the third time, 'Simon son of John, do you love me?' Peter felt hurt because he said to him the third time, 'Do you love me?' And he said to him, 'Lord, you know everything; you know that I love you.' Jesus said to him, 'Feed my sheep.' "

(*The bright lights go off, leaving the room in candlelight.*)

Say: "Peter had the chance to respond again to Jesus' love. We have that chance too. No matter how many times we feel we betray Christ, he is always giving us another chance, asking us, 'Do you love me?'

"We will remove the blindfolds and begin singing our first song for the catacomb worship service." (See page 144.)

# *Romans and Christians*

## The Object of the Game

Romans and Christians is a simulation game that usually takes at least two hours to introduce, play, and debrief. If you include the option for the Catacomb worship, you need to allow three hours. This game attempts to recreate an actual historical situation that the early Church faced during the first few centuries of its existence.

The object of the game is to set up a situation in which participants are faced with a conflict between Christian values and non-Christian values. They are put into a situation in which they have to make decisions about their faith and about what they will or will not do.

At the end of the game, during the debriefing, you will have a chance to deal with direct parallels in today's world for the contemporary Christian.

During the game, the Romans will attempt to destroy the Christian movement by arresting all Christians and either converting them to the Roman faith or putting them in jail or to death. The Christians will attempt to avoid arrest and find their way to the Catacombs, where they can worship God with other Christians.

The game is played as a form of tag. Once a Roman tags a Christian, the Christian is arrested. The Christian cannot resist or run away.

The game can be very intense and emotional and needs to be carefully set up and debriefed.

## The Historical Situation

Beginning in the middle of the first century, Roman emperors began to claim the title of "god." Loyal Roman citizens were expected to worship the emperor as a god and burn incense on an altar. Worship of any other god was held to be treason against the state and was punishable by imprisonment or death.

Suspected Christians were brought before the altar, asked to renounce Christ, and worship Caesar as god. If they did this, they were held to be loyal citizens. If they did not, they were convicted of treason and sent to prison or were put to death. During the early centuries, many thousands of Christians lost their lives in this way.

Some Christians would pretend to worship Caesar and burn incense but would later claim that they did not mean it. This created a crisis in the church. People who had friends and relatives who lost their lives did not want these people in the church. Christians who did burn incense on the altar of Caesar often had to face the anger of other Christians.

To encourage loyal citizens to turn in suspected traitors, Rome passed a law that gave the property of convicted traitors to those who turned them in. The result was that being a Christian was a very serious matter. It was literally a matter of life and death. If the wrong person discovered that you were a Christian, it could cost you your life. It could also cost your family their lives.

To protect themselves, Christians began to develop secret signs and meet in secret places. Roman law forbade the burial of anyone above ground in Rome. Underneath Rome were miles of tunnels, carved out of the soft tuba rock, that were used as underground cemeteries. These were called the catacombs. Christians never lived here, but they arranged to meet and worship in secret in the tunnels and chambers. If the Romans came, they could run away down any number of side tunnels. However, sometimes Christians were captured and killed in the catacombs.

## How the Game Is Played

**Before the Game:** Choose six people (5 adults and 1 youth) and give them their roles. The youth will be the "Catacomb Christian." This is the only person who knows the location of the catacombs at the beginning of the game. This person will be a Christian no matter what slip he or she draws later.

The other five are adults who are Romans with special duties. Two will be priests of Caesar at the Altar to Caesar. They are to take their role seriously and create an atmosphere of dread. Two other adults will be the guards at the Roman Prison. Like the priests, they are to take their role seriously. The fifth adult is the attendant at the Execution Room. This adult stays with those who have to be "executed" (removed from the game).

Count the number of youth who will be playing and then make an equal number of slips of paper labeled *Roman* and *Christian*. Have all the participants file by and take a slip. They are to read the slip and immediately destroy it. They are not to tell anyone what slip they drew. Adults will have special roles as explained below.

After everyone knows whether he or she is a Roman or a Christian, read the historical background and then go over the instructions carefully. Outline the boundaries where the game will be played. The area should be as large as possible. An entire campground, covering several acres, is not too large. Allow time for questions, but limit the time. Take only about 30 minutes to set up the game before you begin play.

Note: All participants hear the instructions to each group.

## Instructions to the Christians

**Physical Setup:** Christians will have only one physical place—the Catacombs. Only one Christian will know the location of this place at the beginning of the game.

The Catacomb Christian will attempt to find several other Christians and let them know the location of the Catacombs. This person will have to be very careful. If the location of the Catacombs is revealed to a Roman, the Christian community could be destroyed. Afterward, the Catacomb Christian will go to the location of the Catacombs for the remainder of the game and wait for other Christians.

The location of the Catacombs can be changed at any time—but only by the Catacomb Christian. This may become necessary if the Romans discover the location of the Catacombs. The Catacombs can be located anywhere in the playing area— even right under the Romans' noses.

**Playing the Game:** Christians want to avoid being arrested and also want to worship Jesus as the one true God. To do this, they will try to find the location of the Catacombs and make their way to it so that they can worship with other Christians.

If possible, they want to convert Romans to the Christian faith. To do this, they can witness to their own faith. This can be dangerous; but even in prison, a Christian can tell about his or her faith.

If a Christian knows where the Catacombs are located, he or she will try to give this information to other Christians. This is dangerous. At the beginning of the game, no one knows who is a Roman or who is a Christian. A person who says that he or she is a Christian may, in fact, be a Roman pretending to be a Christian. Christians try to keep the Romans from finding out the location of the Catacombs. Discovery of the Catacombs by the Romans could result in the deaths of family and friends.

Christians can use a secret sign to identify one another. The Catacomb Christian may want to create such a sign and give it to other Christians so that they can recognize one another. However, if a Roman discovers the sign, it could be used to trick Christians. Christians can attempt to break other Christians out of jail.

If captured, a Christian must decide what to do when taken to the altar. He or she may do one of the following:

1. Refuse to renounce Christ and worship Caesar, and go to jail.
   - While in jail, he or she may try to break out and warn other Christians of the identity of some of the Romans.
   - In jail, he or she may choose to remain for secret purposes, including witnessing to the Roman guards and trying to convert them. If a Christian takes this choice, he or she runs the risk of being executed (removed from the game).
2. He or she may renounce Christ and become a Roman. If the Christian does this, he or she will be given "the mark of Caesar" to demonstrate his or her loyalty.
3. He or she may pretend to renounce Christ in order to get free and warn other Christians of the identity of the Romans.
   - If a Christian does this, he or she will have to live with the permanent "mark of Caesar" and the reaction of other Christians to it.
   - If a Christian renounces Christ and receives the mark of Caesar and is later recaptured, the Roman priests have the right to order his or her execution (removal from the game). He or she is then taken to the Execution Room. (To do this, however, the priests must be convinced by the arresting Roman that the person is, in fact, a Christian.)

   Note: It is possible for a Roman to be executed due to mistaken identity.

4. A Christian can pretend to be a Roman.

## Instructions to the Romans

**Physical Setup:** The Romans have three physical locations set up in the game:

1. The Altar to Caesar—This will be a room in which an altar has been erected. On the altar will be a candle. The seal of Rome is two olive branches forming a circle, with the letters S P Q R in the center. The priests will also need extra candles so that suspected Christians can be made to burn incense to Caesar. The only people allowed in the altar area are the priests and the Romans with their prisoners.
2. The Roman Jail—Roman priests have the right to order anyone to be taken to jail. They also have the right to order the execution of anyone. The jail can be

made of tables set in the center of the room. The jail should be large enough to hold most of the Christians in the game, yet small enough that the Romans can usually stop Christians from escaping. A Christian can escape by hopping over the table. If a Christian can make it 10 feet from the table without being tagged by a Roman guard, then he or she is free. If he or she is tagged, the Christian has to return to the jail for five minutes before he or she can make another attempt. Christians who are not in jail can go to the jail and distract the guards so that other Christians can escape. If these outside Christians are tagged by the Roman guards, they are in jail for a minimum of 15 minutes before they can attempt escape.

Escape should be possible but not easy. If the game involves a large number of people and requires a large jail, you may want to use four guards (one on each side). You may want to mark the 10-foot freedom line with tape on the floor or ground.

Roman guards at the jail have the right to execute anyone in prison if they are provoked. The adult guards should not be easily provoked. But the threat of execution and an occasional execution will keep the mood in the jail from becoming too casual.

3. The Execution Room—Participants are placed in this room either by adults who have removed them from the game or by one of the Roman priests or guards who have had an individual executed. Once a person is removed or executed, he or she is out of the game for the rest of the game.

3. The Debriefing Room—This is where all those who have been executed go later. Anyone who does not want to play the game or who finds playing the game too intense to continue may also go to this room. Adults will be present in this room to debrief the experience and deal with any emotional or faith issues that emerge.

**Playing the Game:** Romans want to eliminate the Christian movement, which is illegal and a threat to the state. They can arrest any participant they think might be a Christian by tagging him or her. They may not tag the adults; however, they can tag another Roman. A true Roman should not mind being taken to the altar. In fact, a true Roman should be eager to prove his or her loyalty.

Once a person is tagged, he or she cannot run away or make any attempt to escape. Anyone attempting to do this is executed on the spot and sent to the Execution Room. Suspected Christians are taken to the Altar of Caesar and asked to renounce Christ and worship Caesar as god. They do this by lighting a candle from the candle on the altar and saying: "Only Caesar is god."

If a person does this, he or she is considered a loyal Roman citizen and allowed to go free. As a sign of loyalty to Rome, he or she is given the Mark of Caesar (No one but the two adult priests are to know what this sign is at the beginning of the game. It is: *666*. This mark should be placed on the body in a location where it cannot be readily seen but can be checked by the priests (for example, on the bottom side of the upper arm). If a person refuses to worship Caesar, he or she is taken to the jail by the arresting Roman. That Roman then goes out in search of more Christians.

Note: Romans can convert and become Christians.

## Adults' Roles

The adults have two jobs in the game:

1. They are to make sure that no one gets so carried away that someone is hurt or that anyone is treated in an unacceptable way. Romans and Christians is a game. The adults will ensure that it remains so. That is why five adults run the Altar, the Jail, and the Execution Room. Adults have the right to put a player out of the game for 10 minutes if he or she is too rough. Repeated infractions will result in a person being put out of the game by the adult.
2. The adults are also to observe what is going on during the game—how the game develops, what happens, what doesn't happen, and so forth. During the debriefing, the adults will report what they have seen.

## How the Game Begins

After the guidelines have been read and there is a brief time for questions, the lights will be dimmed. One of the adult Roman priests will stand before the group and read a decree by Caesar announcing:

## *A Decree by Caesar*

Be it known to all loyal Roman citizens: From this moment on, Caesar is to be worshiped as god. Anyone who worships any other god is guilty of treason. It is the duty of all loyal Roman citizens to seek out those who are disloyal to the state. Anyone suspected of worshiping any other god will be arrested and brought to the Temple and the Altar of Caesar. It has come to the attention of the state that there is a new religious sect called "Christians." This group has shown its disregard and contempt for Caesar and continues to worship their leader, called Jesus, as a god. Citizens, it is your duty to crush this movement.

Tell the participants that they have three minutes until the game begins. Begin the game with a loud noise (a bell, a car horn, and so on) that can be heard by everyone.

## How the Game Ends

The game ends when

1. all Christians have been eliminated by being converted to Romans or by being executed.
2. all Romans have been converted to the Christian faith.
3. or, more likely, when the time limit runs out (usually 1 hour).

At the end of the game, sound the same noise that began the game. Have everyone gather in a predetermined place for the debriefing.

## Debrief

When everyone has reassembled, take about 30 minutes to debrief the exercise. Use the following questions to guide the discussion. Try to get several responses to each question.

**To Everyone:**
• What was the game like for you?
• Were you able to get into your role? Why or why not?

**To the Christians:**
• What happened when the game first began?
• What happened when you were brought before the Altar?
• How did the game develop?
• How many of you lied during the game? Why did you lie or not lie?
• How many of you were willing to light the candle? Why did you do this?
• How many of you refused to light the candle? Why? How did you feel about those who lit the candle?

**To the Catacomb Christian:**
• What did you do?
• What happened?
• How many Christians were executed? How did you feel about that?

**To the Romans:**
• How did the game begin for you?
• How did you identify the Christians?
• How did you feel about arresting and bringing Christians to the altar?
• What was it like being a Roman?

**To the Adults Who Were Wandering Around:**
• What did you notice or observe?
• How did the game develop?
• Did anything concern you?

**To the Adults at the Jail and the Execution Room:**
• What did you notice or observe?
• What did the Christians try to do?
• Did any Christians attempt to witness to you? How effective was their witness?

**To the Adults at the Altar:**
• What was it like playing your role?
• What did you do?
• What did you notice about the people brought before you?

**To Everyone:**
• Why did we play this game?
• What does it have to do with our faith?
• What did you learn?
• What did you learn about yourself?
• What did you learn about others?
• If you were confronted with a direct challenge to your faith, what would you do?

# *Catacomb Worship*

Follow Peter's Walk or Romans and Christians with a Catacomb Worship service, or use by itself or as a closing to a retreat or lock-in. This candlelight service attempts to recreate the worship experience of the early Church.

Before entering the worship area, say:

"Catacomb Worship is a powerful worship experience that seeks to recreate what it was like to worship in the early church. Often the leaders were in prison. There were no Bibles, songbooks, or other resources. Often the early Christians had only one another. This service will recreate this experience in a small dark room, lit only by candles. Plan to sing songs from memory. Plan to pray for one another. Plan to offer Scripture from memory. Prepare for a powerful—and often emotional—worship service."

Have the participants link hands and make a human chain, as they silently walk to the worship area. The worship area will have no lights other than candles. Set up an altar area (with Communion elements, if possible).

For the catacomb service, there are no songbooks or Bibles—nothing printed. The participants' memories are the only resources that can be used during the service.

Use the following order of worship. Ask the participants to suggest hymns to sing and to tell what they have heard and remember of God's Word. For the sermon, have the youth give personal testimonies of what their faith means to them or any other word they feel led to express.

## Order of Service

**Singing of Hymns (several from memory)**
**Opening Prayer**
**Prayers and Concerns**
**Hearing the Word of the Lord**
- stories from the life of Jesus
- teaching from the apostles (Paul, and so forth)
- other Scripture verses (If someone begins a Scripture and cannot finish, someone else can finish it or add to it.)

**The Word of Exhortation**
- spoken by anyone as led by the Spirit of God. (Allow time for several youth to speak. Allow time for silence.)

**The Lord's Supper**
- Sing during Communion.
- Have the participants serve one another the bread and juice.

**Closing Song**
**Closing Prayer/Benediction** (Ask for a volunteer.)

# *Trust Village*

Trust Village is a series of trust exercises that begins with activities that require little trust and then gradually build up to ones that require more. Most of the exercises work best with a small youth group. If your group is larger than ten persons, you will want them to work in smaller teams.

**Preparation:** Have on hand tables and chairs for the triple chair drop exercise. They will need to be against the wall, ready to use. You'll need one table and four chairs for every two small groups. Make sure that the tables and the chairs are strong and stable and that they can take the weight.

**Objective:** To build trust with one another and to explore the importance of trust.

## Explanation of Trust Village

Begin by explaining Trust Village. Then lead the group through the experience. During most of the time, the youth will be doing activities in small groups as the leader guides everyone. Tell the group that the exercises are "challenge by choice"—no one is required to take the risks. Do not allow the group to pressure anyone. Instead, constantly remind the group and each of its members that they may choose to do the challenge or not. But also emphasize the benefits of taking the challenges. Often a person will watch several others participate—including those who weigh more than he or she does—and then decide to go.

Here is the order of activities:

1. Relaxing on the Floor
2. Guided Fantasy to a Place Called Trust Village
3. Nonverbal Greeting of the Inhabitants of Trust Village (With Eyes)
4. Nonverbal Communication of Feelings (With Backs)
5. Hand Shadowing
6. Pile of Hands
7. Willow in the Wind
8. Log Toss
9. Falling Leaf
10. Triple Chair Drop
11. Debrief Trust Village

## 1. Relaxing on the Floor

Subdue the lighting. Then have the youth lie on the floor in a comfortable position so that they are not touching one another. Tell the group that the entire exercise is to be nonverbal. Speaking is not permitted, only listening and participating. You may invite the group members to "keep the quiet" if they hear talking. Remind them that the more they put into this exercise, the more they will get out of it.

Have the participants take several deep breaths, then slowly tighten and release the muscles in various parts of their body, starting with the toes and slowly moving to the head. This exercise should take about five minutes.

**145**

## 2. Guided Fantasy to a Place Called Trust Village

Once the youth have relaxed, take them on a guided fantasy, with their eyes closed. Have the group members imagine being in a forest. Let them use each of their senses. Then have them slowly walk up a hill, through a cave, look over a village in a valley, walk down to the village, enter the village at night, lie down and go to sleep. This should take about five to seven minutes.

## 3. Nonverbal Greeting of the Inhabitants of Trust Village (With Eyes)

Have the youth awaken in the morning and prop themselves up on one arm. Welcome them to Trust Village. Tell them that the people of Trust Village are different from us. They cannot speak. But they have other ways to communicate. Tell them that they are going to greet one another Trust Village-style while keeping the quiet. Have the class members wander around and just look at people's eyes as they walk past.

## 4. Nonverbal Communication of Feelings (With Backs)

Ask the youth what they can tell about each person on the basis of his or her eyes. Have them find a partner and stand back to back. Those who still do not have a partner should raise their hands so that they can find each other. The partners are to greet each other nonverbally, using their backs. Then have them express each of the following emotions, using only their backs:

- "I'm shy."
- "No. I'm not shy."
- "I'm angry."
- "I'm sorry."

Suggest other emotions to express. Then have the youth say, "Goodbye, partner," using only their backs. Have the youth walk around and find a new partner.

## 5. Hand Shadowing

Have one partner hold his or her hands up at about shoulder height with palms up facing the other person. The other partner is to place his or her hands in an exact mirror position one inch in front of the other's palms. Then have the partners nonverbally choose a leader. The leader is to slowly move his or her hands up and down, back and forth, as the partner tries to shadow the movements and stay exactly one inch away. After the youth have done this for about thirty seconds or so, have them trade roles. Then trade back and have them begin to move three-dimensionally, adding moving toward and away from each other's bodies.

## 6. Pile of Hands

Reassemble the small groups and have the members of each one form a circle. Have them place their hands on the floor so that their thumbs are touching each other and their outer fingers are touching the outer fingers of the person on either side of them. You should have a circle of hands. Then have the group slowly begin to inch their hands toward the center. As they come closer, they will have to slowly pile up on one another. Continue this until the entire group has one big pile of hands. The person whose hand is on the bottom, pulls his or her hand out and takes it to the top.

This movement causes a new person's hand to be on the bottom. This person pulls his or her hand out and goes to the top. This continues for a couple of minutes with each person's hands slowly moving down through the pile. Then have the group reverse and slowly move their hands apart until they are back in the original circle.

## 7. Willow in the Wind

The group stands and forms a tight circle with their hands in front, palms flat, near their chests. A volunteer steps to the center. This person closes his or her eyes, folds his or her arms across the chest, and stands rigid.

When the group is ready, the volunteer drops back about six inches to be caught by the group. The person is then gently passed around the circle, like a willow tree being gently blown in the wind. During the exercise the volunteer will keep his or her body rigid and pivot only at the ankles. The volunteer's feet should never move. The volunteer also does not bend at the knees or waist. The volunteer pivots only at the ankles. The rest of the body is rigid.

*Caution:* Several persons should be supporting the volunteer at all times. Have the participants lightly place their hands on the volunteer's shoulders. He or she may be gently and slowly passed around and back and forth for about thirty seconds. Then the person is returned to the center upright and told to open his or her eyes. Repeat with other volunteers. The adults may also be passed around by the group.

## 8. Log Toss

This exercise is similar to the last one, except that the group forms two semicircles—one in front of the volunteer and one behind. Seen from above, the formation would look like two horseshoes facing with the open ends toward each other. Have the volunteer make sure the other group members are ready before falling back (Volunteer: "Ready?" Group: "Ready!" Volunteer: "Falling." Group: "Fall on!"). These commands are important because they establish a contract between the volunteer and the group.

The volunteer falls back about six inches and is gently caught and sent forward to be caught by the group in front (about six inches forward). Then the volunteer is passed back to fall about one foot; then forward one foot; then back two feet; and forward two feet. As in the first exercise, the person's body is rigid and the volunteer pivots only at the ankles—like a log being gently tossed back and forth. Repeat the process with each person in the group who is willing to go, including adults.

## 9. Falling Leaf

In this exercise, the volunteer stands while the group forms two lines behind him or her. The volunteer makes the falling contract with the group, crosses his or her arms, closes his or her eyes, and then falls back while the group catches the volunteer. Then the group raises the volunteer horizontally as high as the smallest member of the group can reach.

The group then gently swings the volunteer back and forth like a falling leaf and slowly lowers the person to the floor. Long, slow swings are best.

This exercise should not be hurried. The person should have to guess where the floor is and when he or she will get there. Make sure that the volunteer's head is held level. Crossing the legs at the ankles makes the legs more stable. The entire body should also be kept level throughout the entire experience.

Begin with the lightest member of the group and gradually work up to the heavier members, repeating with each person. Have the adults in your group do the exercise if the group is physically able and the adults are willing. If you need help with some members or with the adults in your group, recruit additional persons.

## 10. Triple Chair Drop

Each person can do three drops. The first drop is with the person standing in a chair and the group kneeling. Although this is the lowest drop, it is also the most dangerous, due to the closeness to the floor. Take special care to protect the head and upper body. Err on the side of caution. Catch the person higher than you think is necessary.

The second drop will be done with the person standing on the table and the group standing.

The third drop will be done with the person standing on a chair on top of a table and the group standing.

The volunteer is going to make the verbal contract with the group (page 147), then fall backward in a stiff, rigid position and have the group catch him or her. The group holds their arms in a "zipper" formation; they do not link arms.

There is a danger if the volunteer "sits" as he or she falls. This places all the weight in one spot and makes it difficult to catch the person. If the person is flat and rigid, the weight is distributed and the person is easy to catch.

Again, start with the lightest members and work up to the heavier members. With heavier youth and adults, make sure you have enough large people and strength to safely catch the person falling. Recruit help from other groups if you need to. Never attempt a trust fall unless you are sure of safety.

## 11. Debrief Trust Village

Trust Village is a powerful set of exercises and wonderful discussion can come out of it. These questions can help you debrief the experience. Add any other questions that seem appropriate.

- What was this experience like for you?
- What part was the most fun?
- What part was the scariest?
- What was it like for you to trust the group with your physical safety?
- What would it be like to trust this group with your emotional safety?
- How do you feel about our group right now?

# Lifeline/Unseen Hands

The purpose of these activities is to help the group members see their faith (God, Christ, what they have been taught, the Bible) as a lifeline that can get them through life and to see the Holy Spirit as the "unseen hands" that guide us.

**Core Teaching:** Our faith can help guide us in those moments when we cannot see and the Holy Spirit provides guidance for us in those moments.

### John 8:12
Again Jesus spoke to them, saying, "I am the light of the world. Whoever follows me will never walk in darkness but will have the light of life."

### 1 John 1:4-7
We are writing these things so that our joy may be complete.
This is the message we have heard from him and proclaim to you, that God is light and in him there is no darkness at all. If we say that we have fellowship with him while we are walking in darkness, we lie and do not do what is true; but if we walk in the light as he himself is in the light, we have fellowship with one another, and the blood of Jesus his Son cleanses us from all sin.

**Preparation:** *Make sure that you have enough adult leaders for these exercises. You will need at least one adult leader for every group of five youth. If two adults per group are available, use them. Provide "ropes" (yarn) for each group. Have on hand blindfolds for each person.*

One adult from each group will set up a course with the yarn, tying it to trees and bushes and other obstacles. Make the course complicated. It can cross over itself several times, wrap around trees, and so on. Use the whole skein of yarn, or two (each group should have at least one).

Briefly introduce the activities. Say: "An important part of our faith journey involves trust. In this session we will be doing three activities that require trust. In all three activities the group will be blindfolded. We will do a blind trust walk, then two other exercises. After the exercises we will come back and debrief the experience."

## Trust Walk
Blindfold the youth, then have them hold hands as you take them on a blind trust walk to the location of the lifeline. Say: "Go slowly. As you go, tell the person behind you what's coming up ('we're going down a little hill, there are three steps," and so on) and have him or her pass on the information to the next person in line."

## Lifeline
If possible, conduct this exercise with two groups at a time. Have the group leaders find a partner group. Guide the youth to the course that was constructed with yarn. Use the adult and youth leaders to place people on the lifeline (the yarn), guide them,

and take them off the lifeline. Debrief the exercise either as a combined group or as individual groups.

Make sure that you have a person to place the group on the lifeline, someone else to take them off, and a person to monitor the participants on the lifeline. Each youth will be blindfolded and led to his or her course. Give these instructions:

"This is your lifeline. You need to do these three things:

1. Follow your lifeline wherever it leads you.
2. Whatever you do, do not let go of your lifeline, not even for a second. Always maintain contact with your lifeline. You will know when you come to the end.
3. Be careful. You may encounter obstacles along the path that you could trip over or run into.

Start each person individually at the beginning of the course. The participants are to follow the yarn on their own, without any guidance. It's OK if they start going in reverse, or stop, and so on. These kinds of things can happen to us in life. Station an adult at the end of the course to stop the youth and take off their blindfolds. Do not debrief after this exercise; go immediately into "unseen hands."

## Unseen Hands

Repeat the Lifeline activity, with this change. Place two or three obstacles (a chair, and so forth) on the lifeline course. Station one leader by each obstacle. Place the group members on the same course you were just on, but with a twist. This time, start them in the opposite direction so that they are unfamiliar with the course.

As a group member is about to collide with an obstacle, have the leader reach out and gently touch him or her but say nothing. The instinctive reaction is to reach out and feel what is there. In this way, the participants will discover the obstacles and go around them. The leader is not to say anything even if the group members attempt to speak to them.

## Debrief

Have the group go back to its meeting location and debrief the three experiences. Use the following questions to guide the discussion:

### Trust Walk
- What was the trust walk like for you?
- Was the trust walk easy or difficult?
- What made the trust walk difficult?
- How hard was it to trust in the exercise?
- Where is it hard to trust in life?

### Lifeline
- What was the lifeline experience like for you?
- Did you have any difficulties? If so, what were they?
- What enabled you to successfully complete the course?
- How did you know you were at the end?

- What kinds of things form our lifeline in life? (What do we hang on to or use to guide us?)
- What kinds of things form our lifeline as Christians?
- How might God be a lifeline in our lives? How might the Bible?

**Unseen Hands**
- What was the last exercise like for you?
- What happened when you were touched?
- How were you able to use the touch?
- Has a similar experience ever happened to you in your life?
- How does God guide us and/or warn us with unseen hands?

Ask:
- What do all of these exercises have to do with being a Christian?
- What do they have to do with our class?

## Faith Link
Have volunteers read aloud the Scripture passages (John 8:12 and 1 John 1:4-7).

Ask:
- In today's world what kinds of "darkness" do people walk in?
- How can Jesus (or God) help us walk in the light?

End the session with a brief prayer.

# *The Shepherd's Voice*

The purpose of this activity is to help class members understand and appreciate the importance of listening to God's voice as it comes to us through Jesus of Nazareth.

**Core Teaching:** For Christians, Jesus is our Good Shepherd—the one we trust, the one whose voice we listen to, the one who guides us into what is true and right. Discerning Jesus' voice from that of others is a key part of our discipleship.

### John 10:6-18

⁶ Jesus used this figure of speech with them, but they did not understand what he was saying to them.

⁷ So again Jesus said to them, "Very truly, I tell you, I am the gate for the sheep. ⁸ All who came before me are thieves and bandits; but the sheep did not listen to them. ⁹ I am the gate. Whoever enters by me will be saved, and will come in and go out and find pasture. ¹⁰ The thief comes only to steal and kill and destroy. I came that they may have life, and have it abundantly.

¹¹ "I am the good shepherd. The good shepherd lays down his life for the sheep. ¹² The hired hand, who is not the shepherd and does not own the sheep, sees the wolf coming and leaves the sheep and runs away—and the wolf snatches them and scatters them. ¹³ The hired hand runs away because a hired hand does not care for the sheep. ¹⁴ I am the good shepherd. I know my own and my own know me, ¹⁵ just as the Father knows me and I know the Father. And I lay down my life for the sheep. ¹⁶ I have other sheep that do not belong to this fold. I must bring them also, and they will listen to my voice. So there will be one flock, one shepherd. ¹⁷ For this reason the Father loves me, because I lay down my life in order to take it up again. ¹⁸ No one takes it from me, but I lay it down of my own accord. I have power to lay it down, and I have power to take it up again. I have received this command from my Father."

### Psalm 23

¹ The LORD is my shepherd, I shall not want. ² He makes me lie down in green pastures; he leads me beside still waters; ³ he restores my soul. He leads me in right paths for his name's sake.

⁴ Even though I walk through the darkest valley, I fear no evil; for you are with me; your rod and your staff—they comfort me.

⁵ You prepare a table before me in the presence of my enemies; you anoint my head with oil; my cup overflows. ⁶ Surely goodness and mercy shall follow me all the days of my life, and I shall dwell in the house of the LORD my whole life long.

**Preparation:** *Provide blindfolds and a variety of obstacles (yarn, bungees, chairs, and so on) for the journey. Set up a course outdoors or clear a path in a room lengthwise from wall to wall. Place several obstacles in the center of the path.*

Designate one person as the Lost Lamb, another as the Shepherd, and a third as the Wolf. Designate the rest of the group as Noise. The Noise will talk, chat, make "noise," but will not deliberately try to lead the Lamb off the course. The Wolf, on the other hand, will deliberately try to lead the Lamb astray. If the Wolf can confuse the Lamb enough so that the Lamb walks to where the Wolf is, the Wolf has "lunch."

Blindfold the Lamb and have him or her stand at one end of the room. Have the other group members (Shepherd, Noise, and Wolf) stand at the other end of the room. Tell the group that the object is for the Shepherd to guide the blindfolded person safely to the other side of the room so that the Lamb does not hit any of the obstacles or get caught by the Wolf.

The Shepherd is to give the Lamb instructions. The Wolf is to give false instructions or try to cover up the voice of the Shepherd. The Shepherd can move anywhere in the room to give his or her instructions, but cannot get closer to the Lamb than six feet and must keep his or her voice at a normal conversational level. The Wolf has to remain on the opposite wall but can speak loudly. Those playing the part of Noise can travel anywhere, but can speak only in a normal talking voice. In addition, Noise cannot speak directly to the Lamb. Noise's statements and conversation must be about other topics.

Do this activity two times. The first time, have the Shepherd be someone who least knows the person playing the Lamb. Let the Lamb hear the Shepherd's voice one time, without being obstructed. Then begin.

Repeat the activity, this time having someone the Lamb knows well be the Shepherd. Allow the two of them 30 seconds to get together so that the Lamb can try to memorize the Shepherd's voice.

If time allows, you may want to repeat the exercise a couple of times, switching the roles each time. Ideally, have each member of the group play each of the three roles.

## Debrief

Have the group sit in a circle. Ask those who played the Lamb:
- What was that like for you?
- What made the exercise difficult?
- What enabled you to cross the room safely?
- How difficult was it to trust the voice of the Shepherd?
- How distracting were the other voices?
- Was the Wolf able to trick you in any way?

## Faith Link

Have volunteers read aloud John 10:6-18 and Psalm 23. Then ask:

- What is the Scripture trying to say by referring to God or Jesus as a shepherd?
- What insights do these passages give you into the nature of God or Jesus?
- What insights does this exercise give you into hearing God's voice in our lives?
- Have you ever had an experience that you would call "hearing God's voice"? If so, briefly tell about it.
- If God were speaking to you, how would you recognize the voice as God's?
- What is the key to being able to sort out God's voice from other voices?
- What kinds of things in your life do you experience as Noise?
- What kinds of things in your life do you experience as the Wolf?

Close with a prayer.

# *Abraham's Journey*

The purpose of this activity is to have the class members experience what it is like to trust someone to guide them through a complicated path when the message is less than totally clear.

**Core Teaching:** Christian discipleship is a journey of faith. It involves trust. It also involves discernment—trying to figure out what God's will is for our life. God's guidance is not always clear. Sometimes we need to interpret what we hear God saying. Understanding the need for discernment will give us a clearer insight into the story of Abraham and into our own walk with God.

### Genesis 12:1-9

[1] Now the LORD said to Abram, "Go from your country and your kindred and your father's house to the land that I will show you. [2] I will make of you a great nation, and I will bless you, and make your name great, so that you will be a blessing. [3] I will bless those who bless you, and the one who curses you I will curse; and in you all the families of the earth shall be blessed."

[4] So Abram went, as the LORD had told him; and Lot went with him. Abram was seventy-five years old when he departed from Haran. [5] Abram took his wife Sarai and his brother's son Lot, and all the possessions that they had gathered, and the persons whom they had acquired in Haran; and they set forth to go to the land of Canaan. When they had come to the land of Canaan, [6] Abram passed through the land to the place at Shechem, to the oak of Moreh. At that time the Canaanites were in the land. [7] Then the LORD appeared to Abram, and said, "To your offspring I will give this land." So he built there an altar to the LORD, who had appeared to him. [8] From there he moved on to the hill country on the east of Bethel, and pitched his tent, with Bethel on the west and Ai on the east; and there he built an altar to the LORD and invoked the name of the LORD. [9] And Abram journeyed on by stages toward the Negeb.

### 1 Samuel 3:1-10

[1] Now the boy Samuel was ministering to the LORD under Eli. The word of the LORD was rare in those days; visions were not widespread.

[2] At that time Eli, whose eyesight had begun to grow dim so that he could not see, was lying down in his room; [3] the lamp of God had not yet gone out, and Samuel was lying down in the temple of the LORD, where the ark of God was. [4] Then the LORD called, "Samuel! Samuel!" and he said, "Here I am!" [5] and ran to Eli, and said, "Here I am, for you called me." But he said, "I did not call; lie down again." So he went and lay down. [6] The LORD called again, "Samuel!" Samuel got up and went to Eli, and said, "Here I am, for you called me." But he said, "I did not call, my son; lie down again." [7] Now Samuel did not yet know the LORD, and the word of the LORD had not yet been revealed to him. [8] The LORD called Samuel again, a third time. And he got up and went to Eli, and said, "Here I am, for you called me." Then Eli perceived that the LORD was calling the boy. [9] Therefore Eli said to Samuel, "Go, lie down; and if he calls you, you shall say, 'Speak, LORD, for your servant is listening.'" So Samuel went and lay down in his place.

[10] Now the LORD came and stood there, calling as before, "Samuel! Samuel!" And Samuel said, "Speak, for your servant is listening."

**Preparation:** *Provide a blindfold for each participant. Choose the route through which you want your "Abrahams" to wander. If the weather is good, consider an outside location. Be sure that the path has plenty of obstacles that the group will need go over, under, around, though, around, and so forth. If you choose to do this activity indoors, use furniture and other available objects to complicate the path. In either case, the path should not be easy. You will also need a sherpa, or guide, for each small group (family) of about eight. Other adults can participate as part of a family.*

Have your group go to a location near where you will be doing Abraham's Journey. Make sure that your leaders understand the exercise and that they are prepared for their roles. Blindfold the family members, then read aloud Genesis 12:1-3.

Then say: "Welcome to Abraham's journey. Today we will be wandering through the wilderness to a place we cannot see. The journey will not be easy; it will have many obstacles. Your group will be journeying together, just as Abraham's family did. Like Abraham, you will have someone to guide you. The guide's voice will safely guide you to your goal. The problem is that God's voice is not always clear or easy to understand. You will have to listen closely and discern God's voice from the other sounds around you. You will also have to figure out what the voice is saying and what it means and then follow it. You have three minutes to organize your group and prepare for the journey."

During the three minutes, assign guides to each group. Remind them that they cannot touch the family that they are leading and that they cannot say anything the group might understand (words, voice inflection, and so on.). The guides can use whistles, clucking, clapping, and so on. The guides are to then go to their groups and establish a means of communication and then use the communication to guide their groups to "the promised land." Allow about 30 minutes for the groups to complete the task. If possible, assign a few adults to act as safety monitors. These individuals will need to shadow the groups and watch for safety issues.

## Debrief

The family groups can debrief either together or individually. One consideration is that each family will probably finish at a different time. So you may want each guide to debrief his or her family. When the family has completed the journey, have the participants sit in a circle and remove their blindfolds. Then ask:

- What was the experience like for you?
- What was difficult about this experience?
- What were the keys to success?
- How difficult was it to know where the instructions were coming from?
- How difficult was it for you to understand the instructions you were receiving?
- How were you able to decipher the meaning of what you were hearing?

## Faith Link

Have a volunteer read aloud Genesis 12:1-9. Then ask:

- What insight does the exercise we just did give you into the Abraham story?
- What did God really ask Abraham to do?
- How hard do you think this was for Abraham?
- How hard would it be for you?
- In real life, how does God's voice and guidance come to us?
- How do we discern God's voice from all of the other voices around us?
- How do we understand what God is saying to us?
- What insights does this exercise give you into your own walk with God?

Have a volunteer read aloud 1 Samuel 3:1-10. Then ask:

- How did Samuel finally figure out that it was God who was speaking to him?
- Who or what plays that role in our own lives?

Close with prayer.

# 3-D Minefield

The purpose of this activity is to help group members understand the responsibility we have to care for one another, including helping one another watch out for and negotiate through the various dangers of life.

**Core Teaching:** We are our brother's and sister's keeper. We are called to help one another and guide others through the dangers of life and faith.

### Ecclesiastes 4:7-10, 12

[7] Again, I saw vanity under the sun: [8] the case of solitary individuals. . . . [9] Two are better than one. . . . [10] For if they fall, one will lift up the other; but woe to one who is alone and falls and does not have another to help. . . . [12] And though one might prevail against another, two will withstand one. A threefold cord is not quickly broken.

**Preparation:** *To create a 3-dimensional minefield, set up a course with (1) objects on the ground, (2) some hanging down from a tree, (3) string and bungee chord strung across the area at weird angles. The area should be fairly large as well as complicated and intense. All of the objects symbolize dangers: mines, booby traps, snares, other things that can hurt and kill.*

Lead your group to the area that you have created. Let the group know that the goal of this activity is for the participants to successfully guide one another through the 3-D minefield. Success means traveling safely across the area without coming in contact with any of the dangers. The process will be further complicated by the fact that many others will be in the minefield at the same time. This fact will provide added obstacles to avoid, added distractions, and an added degree of difficulty. Small teams will be entering from different directions and traveling in opposite directions.

Have each person find a partner, and then blindfold one member of each team. The sighted partner is to lead the blind partner around the course a couple of times, entering at different angles. The goal is to confuse the blindfolded partner so that he or she cannot memorize the path across the minefield. Once the journey has begun, the sighted partner is not to use his or her hands, only the voice. Challenge the youth to go slowly. The goal is a safe and successful transit, not speed.

After each team has finished, have the partners trade roles and do the exercise again. Have the other partner "confuse" the blindfolded partner by walking around the perimeter to a different entry point.

## Debrief

Invite the participants to sit in a circle, and then ask the following questions. Encourage responses from as many youth as possible. Affirm all answers. Ask:

### When We Were Blindfolded
- What was that like for you when you were blindfolded and crossing the minefield?

**157**

- How did it feel not being able to see?
- What was it like listening to someone else's guidance?
- What did you find helpful that your guide did?

### When We Were the Guide
- What was it like for you when you were the guide?
- When you were the guide, what were the keys to helping someone safely through the minefield?
- What made this journey harder?

## Faith Link
Ask:

- What obstacles are we likely to encounter in our life and faith journeys during the next few years?
- How can we help guide one another through these obstacles?
- What have you learned in this exercise that you might be able to apply to the future in both your life journey and your faith journey?
- What is the point of the passage from Ecclesiastes? Is this idea true?
- How can we as a group (a church, a Sunday school class, a youth program, a group of friends who have common beliefs and values) lift up one another in the months and years to come?

Close with prayer.